The Yale Daily News Guide to Succeeding in College

BY **SHAHEENA AHMAD**

Simon & Schuster

Kaplan Books
Published by Kaplan Educational Centers and Simon & Schuster
1230 Avenue of the Americas
New York, NY 10020

Special thanks to Julie Schmidt

Project Editor: Amy Arner Sgarro
Production Coordinator: Gerard Capistrano
Production Editor: Maude Spekes
Managing Editor: Kiernan McGuire
Executive Editor: Del Franz

Manufactured in the United States of America
Published simultaneously in Canada

May 1997

ISBN 0–684–83757–9

Library of Congress Cataloging-in-Publication Data

Ahmad, Shaheena.
    The Yale Daily News Guide to Succeeding In College/ by Shaheena
Ahmad
    p. cm.
    ISBN 0–684–83757–9
    1. College student orientation--United States. 2. Study Skills--
United States. 3. College Students--United States--Conduct of Life.
    I. Yale Daily News. II. Title.
LB2343.32.A35 1997
378'.198—dc21

CONTENTS

To my parents, Rafiq and Sonia Ahmad, with love and thanks

ACKNOWLEDGMENTS

This book would not have been possible without the help, advice, and support of very many people.

Many thanks to Stephane Clare, former *Yale Daily News* editorials editor, who shared her wit and insight in the chapter on the minority experience. Special thanks also to Chris Grosso, former *YDN* managing editor, who wrote the sections on computing in college, and whose constant moral support kept me (somewhat) sane during the writing of this book.

I'm very grateful to the following members of the *YDN* managing board of 1998, who put in considerable research time on short notice for this project: Jonathan Barbour, Shawn Bayern, Way-Fan Chang, Yen Cheong, Akiko Fujikawa, Danny Goldman, Peter Ligh, Marc Lindemann, Michael Lynn, Ali Mohamadi, Sara Schwebel, Kee Won Shin, Rebecca Smullin, Laura Steinhardt, Jake Sullivan and Thomas Tillona. Shawn Bayern, the *YDN*'s current online editor, also spent many hours compiling information for most of the sidebars in this book.

Thanks to everyone who worked to make this project materialize, especially former and current *YDN* editors Noah Kotch and Jake Sullivan, and the *YDN* business boards of 1997 and 1998. Thanks also to the business staff of the *Yale Daily News*, especially Susan Zucker.

My editor, Amy Sgarro, was extremely helpful, supportive, and understanding from day one, in spite of my poorly timed tendency to flake on her.

Thanks to my friends, who contributed so much substantively to this book, and listened to my endless rantings about it without complaint. Special thanks to my roommate, Margaret Costello, for keeping me sane, to Fiona Havers for keeping me caffeinated, and to Rakhi Dhanoa for always being there for me. Thanks also to Noah, Evin, Jeff, and Kevin for all your supportive, insightful phone calls. You guys are the greatest.

Finally, and above all, I'm grateful to my wonderful family, without whom I never would have survived college myself. My parents and grandmother put up with more than they deserved while I worked on this project, my college-bound brother Sharif lent his unique humor to many sections of this book, and my sister Soheila cured my writer's block with the best motivational speeches I've ever heard come out of a ten-year-old.

About the Author

Shaheena Ahmad is a 1997 graduate of Yale University. At Yale, she double-majored in English and Political Science, worked as news editor of the *Yale Daily News* and executive editor of the *Insider's Guide to the Colleges,* and participated in psychology experiments from which she is slowly recovering. She has few plans for the future, but does aspire to a longer bio in a book someday.

INTRODUCTION

A few short months after the envelopes—fat and thin—stop rolling through your mailbox, you'll arrive.

You'll arrive laden with 17 years' worth of accumulated junk, a pair of empty-nesting parents, and a host of anxieties and expectations.

And whether you arrive expecting an intellectual utopia or a bar with a $30,000 cover charge, your first year of college will be defined by the unexpected. Like the Love Boat, college life is exciting and new, filled with new freedoms, responsibilites, and problems. No one's first-year experience is exactly the same, but a lot of freshmen face similar problems and ask similar questions. This book is an attempt to address those issues.

There's a lot to be said for carving your own niche and the experience of making your own mistakes. And a college survival guide is not going to provide all the answers. But if reading this book can save you from making some of the more common first-year missteps, our lives will have attained meaning.

We wish you luck.

A SPECIAL NOTE FOR INTERNATIONAL STUDENTS

Approximately 500,000 international students pursued academic degrees at the undergraduate, graduate, or professional school level at U.S. universities during the 1995–1996 academic year, according to the Institute of International Education's *Open Doors* report. Almost 50 percent of these students were studying for a bachelor's or first university degree. This trend of pursuing higher education in the United States is expected to continue well into the next century. Business, management, engineering, and the physical and life sciences are particularly popular majors for students coming to the United States from other countries.

If you are not from the United States, but are considering attending a U.S. college or university, here's what you'll need to get started:

- If English is not your first language, start there. You'll probably need to take the Test of English as a Foreign Language (TOEFL) and the Test of Written English (TWE), or show some other evidence that you are fully proficient in English in order to complete an academic degree program. Colleges and universities in the United States will differ on what they consider to be an acceptable TOEFL score. A minimum TOEFL score of 550 or better is often expected by the more prestigious and competitive institutions. Because American undergraduate programs require all students to take a certain number of general education courses, all students, even math and computer science students, need to be able to communicate well in spoken and written English.

- You may also need to take the Scholastic Assessment Test (SAT) or the American College Test (ACT). Many undergraduate institutions in the United States require both the SAT and TOEFL of international students.

- There are over 2,700 accredited colleges and universities in the United States, so selecting the correct undergraduate school can be a confusing task for anyone. You will need to get help from a good advisor or at least a good college guide that explains the different types of programs and gives you some information on how to choose wisely. Since admission to many undergraduate programs is quite competitive, you may also want to select three or four colleges and complete applications for each school.

- You should begin the application process at least a year in advance. An increasing number of schools accept applications year round. In any case, find out the application deadlines and plan accordingly. Although September (the fall semester) is the traditional time to begin university study in the United States, at most schools you can also enter in January (the spring semester).

- Finally, you will need to obtain an I-20 Certificate of Eligibility in order to obtain an F-1 Student Visa to study in the United States. This you will request from the university. The school will send you the I-20 document once you have been accepted.

For an overview of the undergraduate admissions process, see the appendix on college admissions in this book. For details about the admissions requirements, curriculum, and other vital information on top colleges and universities, see Kaplan's *Road to College*.

ACCESS AMERICA™

If you need more help with the complex process of undergraduate school admissions and information about the variety of programs available, you may be interested in Kaplan's Access America program.

Kaplan created Access America to assist students and professionals from outside the United States who want to enter the U.S. university system. The program was designed for students who have received the bulk of their primary and secondary education outside the United States in a language other than English. Access America also has programs for obtaining professional certification in the United States. Here's a brief description of some of the help available through Access America.

The TOEFL Plus Program

At the heart of the Access America program is the intensive TOEFL Plus Academic English program. This comprehensive English course prepares students to achieve a high level of proficiency in English in order to successfully complete an academic degree. The TOEFL Plus course combines personalized instruction with guided self-study to help students gain this proficiency in a short time. Certificates of Achievement in English are awarded to certify each student's level of proficiency.

Undergraduate School/SAT Preparation

If your goal is to complete a bachelor of arts (B.A.) or bachelor of science (B.S.) degree in the United States, Kaplan will help you prepare for the SAT or ACT, while helping you understand the American system of education.

Applying to Access America

To get more information, or to apply for admission to any of Kaplan's programs for international students or professionals, you can write to us at:

Kaplan Educational Centers
International Admissions Department
888 Seventh Avenue, New York, NY 10106

Or call us at 1-800-522-7700 from within the United States, or 01-212-262-4980 outside the United States. Our fax number is 01-212-957-1654. Our E-mail address is world@kaplan.com. You can also get more information or even apply through the Internet at http://www.kaplan.com/intl.

INDEPENDENCE DAY

part 1

WHAT TO BRING?

The night before I left to come to college my freshperson year, I began to freak out. Should I bring 17 years' worth of photos? Was it necessary to buy a computer before I got here? Did I need to buy an iron if I had never used one in the past? Deeply philosophical questions like these plagued me as I folded my jeans and shirts into suitcases.

—Junior, Yale University

Packing for college can be more taxing than the SATs and require more stamina than your first all-nighter. Clothes, appliances, furniture, room decorations—figuring out what and how much of it to lug to school can really try your sanity, not to mention that of your parents. The temptation to bring a lifetime of accumulated junk with you to college is a great one, but remember that even if you manage to cram it all into the U-Haul, dorm rooms are often of shoebox proportions. And don't forget—if you're going to be moving everything but the family dog into your new pad, eight months down the line you're going to be stuck moving it out again.

So when it comes to packing, let "less is more" be your mantra. Try to pack only the essentials, and when in doubt, leave it home; you can always ask Mom or Dad to ship the rest later.

> It's always easier to have your parents send you something later then to have to send something back yourself if you don't have room for it. Then you don't have to do the work. Anyway, when you first get to college, your parents are so anxious and miss you so much they'll do pretty much anything.
>
> — Senior, Johns Hopkins University

So here are some of basics—must-have items that you might have forgotten and will wish you hadn't.

CLOTHING

Most people tend to take way too much clothing freshman year. The average college closet (even if you're lucky enough to get one for your very own) will not accommodate every ugly sweater you've ever gotten for Christmas. Take this as an opportunity to go through your closet and weed out anything you don't wear on a fairly regular basis. People tend to dress down in college; lots of pairs of jeans are a must. Pack some semi-formal attire, though, for the many "welcome" functions you'll attend in your first few weeks—freshman dinners, freshman assemblies, etcetera.

Think hard about what the weather's like at your school and pack accordingly. If you're from a warmer climate and are heading for a school up north, this may mean a few shopping trips before you hit the road. One of our next-door neighbors freshman year braved New Haven's numbing cold in her Mississippi miniskirts; it was truly a miracle that she escaped frostbite. If you're heading for a colder climate, it's a good idea to bring the winter coat, since it often gets cold enough to wear it before Thanksgiving break. Also remember "duck" boots or Gore-Tex™ lined foot gear, as well as an umbrella (two if you can swing it, since umbrellas tend to disappear incredibly quickly).

Last, but certainly not least, remember socks and underwear. Lots of it. The more the better. It's always possible (if unappealing) to put off doing laundry until you run out of clean underwear. Although we did hear of one person who just turns it inside out . . . but you don't want to do that.

Speaking of laundry, when you do finally make it to the laundry room, transporting your clothes in a laundry bag rather than a bin or a basket is probably most practical. Sturdy laundry bags are available in most discount stores. If you're truly ambitious, invest in a (really) cheap iron and mini-ironing board. If not, chances are one of your neighbors will have one tucked away, or there might be one available for public use in your dorm's laundry room.

> One thing you can try to do is bring enough clothes for the season and transport wardrobes during vacations or breaks, so you don't have to bring all your clothes at once.
>
> —Sophomore, Boston University

THE BATHROOM

A nice, warm bathrobe and slippers are good to have, since you may be trekking down the hall frequently to get to the bathroom. You might also want to take along a pair of flip-flops for the shower. Yes, bathing in shoes seems somehow unnatural, but so is the grime festering on the floors of many college showers. And don't forget a shower caddy to lug your stuff to the bathroom—the kind with holes for drainage is best. Avoid shower "buckets"; they tend to be a friendly breeding ground for unidentifiable molds and growths.

LINENS

At many schools, the beds require extra-long sheets, 80" rather than the standard 75"—find out the size you'll need before you buy. You should take along at least two sets. Most people opt for comforters and skip the bedspreads, since they let you make your bed in a flash, if you choose to make your bed at all. Dorm mattresses are similar in constitution to those that prisoners sleep on; some kind of washable mattress pad for your bed will make it infinitely more comfortable.

Bring along your favorite pillow, and also look for those armchairlike study pillows—they're great for reading in bed or on a window seat.

APPLIANCES AND FURNITURE

The most crucial thing to do when thinking about what kinds of major appliances and furniture to bring is to consult with your roommate(s).

You should talk at least once during the summer, not only so you can get acquainted before arriving on campus, but also to make sure that your room doesn't end up with two TVs and no refrigerator. Or six Monet prints and nothing to sit on. Talking to your future roomies beforehand can avoid a lot of these hassles and ensure a pretty good setup once you arrive at school.

You can get a pretty good idea of what freshman dorms are like before you arrive by calling the dean's office or current students. Chances are you'll be living in either a single, a double, or a suite consisting of a few bedrooms and a common room or living room. In terms of furniture, most schools provide their students with just the basics: bed, dresser, desk, chair. Obviously, this makes for fairly spartan accommodations. If you're really lucky, your room will come equipped with amenities like a mirror or bookshelves, but if not, you'll have to clean out your bedroom at home and bring these items yourself. If you'll be living in a suite with a living room, heaven has smiled on you; get down on your knees and show your gratitude. Then, after you dust yourself off, start looking for furniture.

Looking for furniture is a lot easier if you've a) coordinated with your roommates, and b) acquired certain information, such as average room measurements, beforehand. If your common space is big enough, you'll need some kind of couch, chairs, a rug, maybe a coffee table. If you have a sibling who just graduated or old furniture tucked away in the garage or basement, life is good. Otherwise, you'll have to get creative to keep from shelling out the big bucks. The Salvation Army and other secondhand or thrift stores are a great place to start—you can often find comfortable furniture in decent condition at rock-bottom prices. If you come up short, hit the summer garage sale circuit. You can also find cheap carpet remnants at furniture outlets or discount warehouses like Caldor or K-Mart. If your dorm room isn't carpeted, a rug is a must; it will warm up your living space better than any other single item. A final note when it comes to actual furniture for your dorm room: If you arrive at school and discover you are in desperate need of a beanbag or a coffee table, there will probably be scores of recent graduates hawking their wares (dirt-cheap) all over campus.

Another thing to consider: Make sure your future home has adequate overhead lighting. Freshman year, we lit our enormous common room with a half-dozen 60 watt desk lamps; we literally saw spots all year. If lighting could be a concern, be kind to your eyes—consider investing in a halogen lamp. They're pricier and uglier than shaded lamps and not as cool as lava lamps, but just one can completely light up an average-sized room. One note of caution—several universities have recently banned halogen lamps, deeming them fire hazards. Check with your school before investing in one.

When it comes to appliances and electronics, there are few must-haves. Obviously, you should make sure someone is bringing a clock and a phone—you'd be surprised how often these particular items are overlooked. You may also need an answering machine, although more and more schools are offering some kind of voice mail option. A small refrigerator is one of the few electrical appliances that is an absolute necessity. Most schools offer some kind of yearly refrigerator rental service, but if you can find a used one and are hoping to spend at least a couple of years in college, it might be cheaper in the long run to buy. Coffee pots, if you need regular caffeine fixes, are also pretty standard. As for other appliances, such as hot plates, microwaves, toasters, and rice cookers, try to gauge realistically how often you will really use these items. Remember that you'll probably be on some kind of full meal plan, and will probably have access to some kind of points system you can use to grab late-night snacks and coffee. An army of random cookware might not be entirely necessary. Also, some schools consider certain electrical appliances fire hazards, and ban them from on-campus rooms.

As for entertainment-type items, most people bring at least some kind of CD player or stereo system from home. You own personal preferences and budget will determine whether you'll need just a box or some kind of full-fledged system. Again, don't neglect to consult with your roomies. When it comes to a TV or VCR, if you have one lying around your house, and your parents don't object, go ahead and take it to school, but it's not a necessity for everyone. In fact, the constant temptation of the tube can prove a dangerous distraction for die-hard junkies or serious procrastinators. If you know you are true TV addict, if given the opportunity you will spend more hours a day watching soap operas than doing reading, do yourself and your GPA a favor—leave the TV at home.

There will probably be some kind of TV lounge just down the hall or in the basement where you can get your weekly fix of *ER*.

COMPUTERS: TO BUY OR NOT TO BUY?

One of the biggest decisions you'll make before you leave for school is whether or not to buy a computer, if you don't already own one. If you can't afford to bring a computer to college, rest assured that most universities provide easy, free access to computers in the form of public computing labs (or clusters, as they're sometimes called). If you can work it into your budget, however, you'll probably want the convenience of having a computer in your room—to type papers, E-mail, or just procrastinate with a nice long session of Super Maze Wars. Computer clusters may be located several blocks from your dorm, and worse, they may become nightmarishly packed during midterm and final periods. Sleep-deprived, bleary-eyed, and facing a quickly approaching deadline, you might not react well to a crowded computer cluster. And a catfight over a keyboard is never a pretty sight.

If you're budget minded, a computer definitely does not have to be a major investment. Many schools offer good deals on new computers, so be sure to check with yours before buying a machine at home. Often, school computing services will be as competitive as the CompUSA around the corner.

Other affordable alternatives include buying a used computer, preferably from someone you know, or buying a new computer, but an older model. You probably won't be using your computer for more than games and word processing, so don't automatically head for the latest, superfast Pentium computer loaded with memory and multimedia features. An older, slower model will get the job done just as well.

Shopping

Before buying a computer, think about what types of things you plan on doing with the machine. If you're planning on writing programs for computer science classes or playing *Doom*, you'll want a fast computer with lots of memory for building programs or blowing up assorted bad guys. If you're not as technologically inclined, you might want to settle for an older, cheaper model. Here are a few things to consider in your quest for a machine that will meet your computing needs without driving you to bankruptcy before you've even arrived at school.

Macs versus PCs

When it comes to the great Macintosh versus PC debate, the best solution is to determine which system would be most convenient at your college. For instance, if Macs are dominant in your school's computing clusters, you might want to purchase a Mac just for convenience's sake. Although Windows 95 has made the PC almost as easy to use as the Mac, Macs are often cheaper and easier to network. The overriding consideration in your decision, though, should be which system is most prevalent at your school.

Desktop versus laptop

After deciding whether you want a Mac or a PC, the next major consideration is whether to buy a desktop or a laptop unit. Desktop units are usually cheaper, more powerful, and have better displays, but a laptop can provide you with more flexibility. With laptops, you can bring your computer to class with you to take notes, or write your paper in the library. Now that they've have dropped in price substantially, laptops are definitely worth considering, especially if you plan on using your computer mostly for word processing.

Speed

Next, you need to decide how fast a computer you'll need. Approach this decision with great skepticism. Do you really need a superfast processor? Remember, even if you buy the fastest processor on the market, your computer will be hopelessly behind the power curve in a few months anyway. Buy the cheapest computer you can find that will run all the software you plan on running. The most common pitfall when it comes to buying a computer is spending too much money on a machine that is far too powerful.

Memory

Besides the processor, you also need to consider how much memory, or RAM, you want. You should get at least eight megabytes to start. If you're interested in saving money, you can usually stop there, and then buy more later. But do not skimp on the hard drive; you'll find that you need that space.

Web access

Think about whether or not you want to reach the Internet from your desktop or laptop. If your school offers network access from your dorm room, make sure you get a computer powerful enough to access the Net. Usually, this means a computer with at least a 486 processor and eight megabytes of RAM.

Also find out what kind of network your college has—the most common type of network is Ethernet. Depending on what kind of computer you buy, you might have to spend up to $200 extra to connect to the school's internal network.

Printing

Will you need to purchase a printer? A good deskjet printer runs about $200 and might be a worthwhile investment. Most schools do offer laser printing at a nominal fee (about 10 cents a page), so a printer is one place you can probably afford to skimp. Another option is to buy a cheap, used printer to print out drafts of papers, and then print your final copies on the school's laser printer. Your best bet is probably to hold off on getting a printer until after you arrive at school, when you can evaluate how accessible and inexpensive printing services are.

Multimedia

Fancy features like CD-ROM drives, speakers, and microphones will probably have little to offer you. Despite the hype, few people use CD-ROM in college to do research, especially if they have convenient Internet access.

A final point about security. Besides your bottle opener, your computer is probably your most valuable possession in college. Protect it. Don't leave your laptop lying around in the library, and don't leave your door open with your computer sitting pretty on your desk. Most schools provide a service that allows you to brand your valuables by etching your license numbers on the computer. Definitely do this as soon as possible. You might also want to take out an inexpensive insurance policy on your computer, just in case your ceiling collapses on it or your roommate douses it in cheap beer.

CHECKLIST

Here are some more detailed suggestions about what to bring with you to college. These are not all necessarily must-have items (obviously, not every one of you will need to pack tampons), but all of them have been known to come in handy:

Clothing
Excessive amounts of socks, underwear, bras, tights, pj's, bathrobe, slippers, T-shirts, jeans, sweatshirts, flannels shorts, bathing suit, workout clothes, sweaters, hats, slacks, sports jacket and ties, dress socks, pantyhose, skirts, dresses, khakies, chinos, snow pants, and shoes (dress, casual, and sneakers).

Bathroom and medicine chest items
Toothpaste, toothbrushes, razors, blades, shaving cream, soap, soap dish, shampoo, conditioner, something to carry it all to the shower in, deodorant, blow dryer, hairbrush, tweezers, nail clipper, nail file, emory boards, brush, mirror, tampons/pads, tissues, cotton balls, Q-tips, TP, glasses, contact solution, prescription medication in original containers, pain relievers such as acetaminophen or ibuprofen, sunblock, moisturizer, band-aids, first-aid kit.

Electronics and appliances
Light bulbs (100, 150, or even 200 watt), halogen lamp, desk lamp, bed lamp, alarm clock, clock/radio, telephone, answering machine, stereo, tapes, CDs, TV, VCR, computer/printer, refrigerator, microwave, can/bottle opener, hotpot, fan, camera, film, 3-2 prong adapters, extension cords, surge protector.

For your bed
Extra-long sheets, pillowcases, pillows, study pillow, comforter, mattress pad, condoms.

Miscellaneous room items
Mirror, bulletin board, bookshelves, wastepaper basket, picture hooks, hammer, nails, screws, Krazy Glue™, stick-on hooks, utensils, plates, cups or mugs, drying rack, iron or ironing board, laundry bag, detergent, closet organizer, clothes basket, hangers, hook for laundry bag.

Desk items and academic supplies

Backpack, pens, pencils, sharpener, notebooks, clipboard, highlighter, memo board for door or desk, envelopes, stamps, stationery, address book, scissors, paper clips, rubber bands, scotch tape, hole puncher, ruler, calculator, pocket and desk calendars, paper (looseleaf/graph), staples, stapler and staple removers, dictionary, thesaurus, style guide, book of quotations.

HELPFUL HINTS FOR PACKING IT ALL UP

With any luck, you'll remember to find or purchase all items crucial to your survival before school starts. Packing your stuff without damaging or destroying anything is yet another story. Whether you're shipping it or piling it into the family sedan, it's important to take some precautions and save yourself the trouble of having to replace those new-found treasures. Here are a few helpful hints for packing.

- Label everything. Obsessively. Compulsively. You'll be glad you did when, your first night at school, you're not forced to open a dozen boxes to find your toothbrush.

- When it comes to packing valuables like your computer, printer, or stereo, try to use the boxes the items originally came in; they'll be a lot safer that way, and the original packing materials will keep these big-ticket items from getting jostled around or damaged en route.

- If you're an efficient packer, suitcases work fine for clothing, but only if you're planning on unpacking your clothes while your parents are still in town so they can take the luggage back with them; otherwise, you'll be stuck trying to find space for three suitcases in a room the size of a shoebox. Cardboard boxes are probably the better bet; if you buy the fold-up kind, you can hide them discreetly under your bed once you move in and drag them out again come moving-out time.

- If you're packing clothes, line the boxes with plastic, and if you're packing anything fragile, buy some bubble wrap to protect them.

- Try to put fragile, valuable items near the middle of the box, and surround them with sweatshirts or something else to pad them.

- Try not to pack open bottles of shampoo, lotions, or make-up. They have an ill-timed tendency to leak, or, if it's really your lucky day, explode. If you must, make sure they're tightly closed and put them in individual plastic bags.

- Don't put all your favorite and/or most valuable belongings in the same box. That will be the box that is lost/stolen/destroyed. Guaranteed.

Once you get to school, don't freak if you realize you've forgotten some important item; chances are you'll find nearby drugstores where you can pick up everyday necessities, and you can always ask your parents to ship other essentials later on. Don't let packing for college be a bigger stress than it needs to be; you have enough stress-inducing tasks waiting for you upon your arrival.

SHIPPING AND TRANSPORTATION

You've planned with your future roommates. You've scoured garage sales and ransacked the aisles of K-Mart. You've packed enough underwear to last you until the turn of the millennium. Just one thing left to do.

Get it all there.

Obviously, transporting yourself and your gear to college will be easiest if you live near enough school that your parents can just load up the car and drive you there. If you'll be cruising the friendly skies, however, you'll have to chart your path a little more carefully and a little further in advance.

AIRPLANE!

If you do end up flying, make your reservation several weeks in advance. Also, keep in mind that the cost of a cab from the airport to your campus can rival tuition, so try make arrangements for transportation before you arrive. Your school may run a free shuttle bus to and from the airport at regular times, or may be able to provide you with information about commercial bus or shuttle services.

When it comes to booking the flight itself, it's probably best to go through a travel agency; doing so won't cost you any more than booking your flight yourself, and the agent can help you find out about special fares, student discounts, and substantially cheaper standby tickets. Your status as a student could entitle you to big savings. Also, if you don't mind traveling at strange hours (late night or early morning), these flights are often cheaper. And finally, if you're willing to get "bumped" from a full flight to a later, less crowded one, many airlines reward you with a voucher redeemable for up to 1,000 free air miles.

When you're heading back home for Thanksgiving, winter, or spring breaks, remember to make your reservations in advance. If your new city has just one small airport, it'll turn into a madhouse as soon as classes end, and you may have a hard time getting on a flight. Consider skipping town as soon as your exams are over, or a couple of days before recess officially begins.

Tips from Students Who Fly

If hitting the road is not an option for you and you'll have to take to the skies, there are a few things you need to keep in mind, besides the fact that your seat can be used as a flotation device. Here are some tips from student flyers:

- "Don't wear metal buckled boots—they tend to set off metal detectors."

- "Keep your ticket stubs—you'll need them to collect your luggage."

- "Stand behind the hot girl/guy on line when getting your ticket. Then ask to sit next to that person when the stewardess does seat assignments."

- "Fly European airlines whenever you are flying from Europe. They don't card for alcohol."

- "Always try to get a night plane out from school so you can spend the day packing. Never underestimate how long it takes to pack."

- "Get on the plane as early as possible when bringing dufflebags onboard. The overhead racks will often fill up quickly if there are a lot of students. Fill up with bags, that is. Not students."

- "Bring a Walkman. It comes in handy if you sit next to someone annoying."

SHIPPING YOUR STUFF

If you are flying to school for the first time, you have few alternatives besides getting your stuff shipped; UPS is probably your best bet. Call your school during the summer and find out when and where UPS shipments should be sent, since you may not be able to receive packages at your personal mailing address. It takes about a week for shipments to arrive, so plan for your boxes to make it there a couple of days before you do.

UPS will generally pick up your boxes at your home, if you call them a day in advance. When you call about pickup, make sure you ask about any special packaging instructions or recommendations. And whatever you do, if you are shipping valuables, insure, insure, insure. A couple of dollars can save you hundreds later if your printer or stereo is destroyed en route, not to mention one massive and poorly timed headache.

> My roommate, who's from California, had lotsa stuff. Lots. As though she were a family of four. And she had to get it all home. Because the airlines only allow you three checked bags or per person, she had to ship it. The plan was to ship as few boxes as possible, which was not such a good plan because someone had to carry those mammoth boxes 'cross the hills and dales (mostly hills) of Providence, and that someone was me. And, of course, the eternal dilemma—UPS or Postal Service—became the sole topic of conversation in our room for weeks and weeks. UPS is four times as expensive, but it arrives; the Postal Service is really, really cheap, but it doesn't. Which we learned when we sent the books UPS and the kitchen stuff USPS, and she had to buy new pots and pans.
>
> — Sophomore, Brown University

You can bring some of your valuables with you on the plane—most carriers allow three suitcases and one piece of carry-on luggage. But suitcases get treated pretty roughly by cargo handlers, and bringing valuables with you on the plane may not be any safer than sending them UPS.

One last word of advice: It's definitely wise to is pack a change of clothes and some toiletries with you in your carry-on bag. You never know—though you may be headed to Stanford, your bags, laden with everything of value that you own, may be destined for Dallas.

HIT THE ROAD

If you live near enough to campus that you can drive or your parents can drive you, your options are considerably wider when it comes to transporting your gear. You can try to cram your boxes into a station wagon, but if everyone but the family dog is going along for the ride, this may not be feasible. Other possibilities include taking two cars and two drivers, or borrowing or renting a minivan. Whatever you decide to do, make sure you have enough room; it's illegal (and not too safe) to drive with the driver's rear view completely obscured.

One of my roommates illustrates perfectly how not to come to school. At the end of each school year he takes all his belongings home with him. At the start of the next school year he brings everything back. Usually his parents drive him the thousand-mile journey in a school-stuff-filled car. On one such trip my roommate's rollerblades, which were tied to the luggage rack on top of the car, fell off somewhere in Western Pennsylvania.

This year he rented a car and drove himself the trek to school. When he arrived, I helped him unload his car. Things were thrown into the car, not in suitcases, not in plastic or paper bags, but just thrown in. Books were crammed under car seats, clothes were dangling from every nook, cranny, and loose metal fixture that was available. Together we must have made about fifty trips to and from the car.

My other roommate illustrates perfectly how to travel to and from school. At the end of the school year, he takes home only what he needs, storing the rest at school, and starting his vacation off on the right foot by relaxing on an airplane watching some cheesy airplane flick instead of being stuck in his car, face compressed to the window because of all the extraneous personal belongings.

—Sophomore, Penn State University

In the end, probably the easiest method of transport for the big move is renting a U-Haul. The price varies depending on how many miles you drive, the size of the trailer, and whether or not you cross state lines, but the convenience may very well outweigh the cost.

If you're planning on driving to school alone, get your car checked out thoroughly before you leave. The next best thing you can do is get yourself a membership in an auto club, such as AAA. Membership in an auto club will run you about $30–$40 a year (often less if your parents are members), but the peace of mind well outweighs the costs. Joining AAA entitles you not only to a variety of nifty maps, but also a wide range of benefits that can pull you out of the depths of car despair 24 hours a day, from a jump-start to a free tow to the nearest gas station. Even if the club charges a nominal fee for a long-distance tow, it doesn't exist to extort money in the same fashion as your typical tow truck company.

YOU'VE MADE IT: DO YOU NEED WHEELS?

Having a car on campus can be both a real advantage and a serious hassle. At some very large schools and on commuter campuses a car is absolutely indispensable. A car can also be useful if your school is a member of an academic consortium or near a number of other colleges or universities, and you expect to do research or socialize regularly on a nearby campus. If you go to school within driving distance from your house, you can travel home (or road trip elsewhere) stress-free during vacations and even on the occasional weekend. And finally, a car can expand your horizons if you go to a school in the boonies, with limited shopping or entertainment immediately surrounding campus.

Despite all these potential benefits, though, the grim reality is that on most campuses, a car can be far more trouble than it's worth. You usually can't drive to your classes, since classroom buildings are typically located off of roads (and in walking distance from dorms anyway), and street parking is strictly limited during the day. Having a car introduces a whole range of extra worries, responsibilities, and expenses into your already stressful life, from maintenance to security to chauffeuring your friends around. So before you bring your baby to campus, ask yourself several questions and evaluate your situation.

- First of all, are you even allowed to have a car on campus? Many schools don't even allow freshmen to register cars — this is information is definitely to know before you drive 500 miles to school solo.

- Secondly, what's the parking situation like? Some schools don't even have their own official student parking lots, which means you either have to risk parking your car in the football stadium lot on a regular basis, or pay possibly exorbitant monthly fees at a local parking garage. Are there secure, well-lit parking lots near campus? Do you have to take a shuttle bus or walk through an unsafe neighborhood to get there? Is there adequate daytime street parking, or will you be subject to the whims and caprices of moody or vindictive meter maids? Parking on many college campus has the potential to turn into a nightmare from which you can never awake.

- Finally, what's the area surrounding your campus like? If everything you need, from a drugstore to a movie theatre, is in walking distance, or easily accessible through cheap and safe public transportation, a car may be an unnecessary expense.

If You Bring Your Car

If you *do* decide to bring your car, here are a few tips to keep it and you secure and running:

- Get your car checked out before you hit campus. If there's anything wrong, you want to take care of it while you're still on familiar territory, as well as get an oil change, check the tires, etcetera.

- If you don't already have an auto club membership, get one. It can save you hundreds on a tow, and rescue your keys from inside your locked car before too many of your friends discover your idiocy.

- Avoid driving around at night by yourself, especially if you're a woman, and park only in well-lit, nonisolated spaces or lots.

- Don't keep valuables in your automobile. And if your radio is detachable, take it with you when you leave your car.

- OK, this should go without saying, but here it it: Follow traffic laws, and never drive when you've been drinking. Even minor traffic violations can boost your likely already too-high insurance premium, and driving when you've been drinking can destroy your life and that of others.

- And finally, don't lend your car to a friend. A lot of students succumb to pressure from friends to borrow their cars. A lot of students are also sorry—nothing sours roommate relations faster than a totaled vehicle. Try, whenever possible, to drive friends where they need to go; if you lend them your car and there's some sort of accident, you'll not only tumble into the insurance inferno, but you may also endanger a perfectly good friendship. So, have a spine, and neither a borrower nor a lender be.

ORIENTATION WEEK

The first week of school, usually called "Orientation Week," is kind of like a carnival: swarms of people milling about aimlessly, mindless activities, everyone treating you nicely—and they don't even want to sell you cotton candy. It's like College Lite—no papers, no tests, no classes, no deadlines. You'll want another one when you're a senior, when you can fully appreciate it. But when you're a freshman, this frenetic week is defined by the extremes of stress and exhilaration. Besides the small matters of leaving behind your family and friends, and meeting the people with whom you'll be sharing the next four years, there are a host of logistical and practical things to take care of: choosing classes, taking placement exams, getting to know campus, buying books, setting up phone service, a P.O. box, E-mail, a bank account . . . it's enough to make your head spin. So here's a step-by-step guide to surviving Orientation Week—and maybe having a decent time while you're at it.

GETTING AROUND CAMPUS

Your dorky map will be indispensable. Don't worry, there will be dozens of other readily identifiable freshman consulting them throughout the first few days of college. Carry it always, and carry it with pride . . . OK, carry it discreetly, but make sure you have it with you at all times. You *will* get lost; it's kind of an inevitability, especially if you're on a big campus, and especially if you have to take any kind of transportation whatsoever to get from one part of campus to another. But there's good news—there will be a lot of freshmen in the same position as you, and it's kind of fun to wander around together and discover campus together. During Orientation Week, make sure you take plenty of time out to explore classroom buildings, dormitories, student centers, the bookstore, the gym, etcetera. In a month, you won't notice the gargoyle statue on the library steps as you race for a study cubicle, a.k.a. weenie bin, so enjoy discovering campus while there's still joy in the discovery. Anyway, it's definitely a good idea to get a handle on where things generally are before classes start; you don't want to head out to a 9 A.M. class (you actually don't want to take a 9 A.M., but we'll get to that later) the first week of classes and realize at 8:55 you've gone four blocks in the wrong direction. So wander. Wander without destination. Wander without purpose . . .

THE NUTS AND BOLTS

OK, scratch that. During Orientation Week, you'll need to wander with a purpose. With many purposes, as a matter of fact. A mountain of drudgery lies ahead you, even beyond what you thought were the insurmountable obligations of unpacking and decorating. Your assignment is to accomplish every stupid-yet-necessary task that lies before you prior to D-Day, day one of classes: You want your phone hooked up, your E-mail account and P.O. box primed to receive all that correspondence from home, your bank account ready to be depleted. You face a difficult and dangerous mission.

Phone hook-up

If you're very lucky, you'll have the option of setting up phone service from home, so you'll be ready to go as soon as you arrive on campus. More likely, you'll have to wait on a long, slow line some time after you arrive for phone installation and voice mail. It usually takes three to five business days before you have a working phone. Be prepared to shell out the big bucks, as well; standard phone service with call waiting and voice mail can cost upwards of $200, split between however many people are living in your suite.

Phone Calls Home: Cheapskating It

When you get to college, you may find that the phone service is unusually expensive. For your first few weeks, you might not care—talking to parents and friends might be worth the high costs. But eventually, high long-distance telephone bills can begin to wear on you.

Fear not. There are several small but reliable telephone companies that offer "calling cards" at reduced rates, with no yearly fees, application charges, or minimum usage requirements. With most of these companies, you risk nothing by calling and applying to get a calling card: since they work just like credit cards, you don't pay until you use them. These calling cards usually work by calling an 800 number, so you can avoid your campus's phone service if it's expensive.

- ATCALL offers something called the "NOBScard" (standing for "NO B.S."). Intended for college students, the NOBScard provides service for 18 cents a minute with no per-call charge nationwide at any time of day. Call (888) 211-NOBS to apply or get more information, or visit their Web site at http://www.atcall.com. (At the time this was written, ATCALL was offering 30 free minutes to those who receive their card.)

- Sprint offers a very reasonable card called the FONCARD. It lets you make calls for only 9 cents per minute between 9 P.M. and 9 A.M. There is, however, an 80-cent surcharge, so it's best for long calls. The FONCARD is free to get, and there's no monthly charge. Like ATCALL, Sprint is offering 30 free minutes to those who receive their card. Call (800) 793-1160 to apply.

- VoiceNet is very similar to the NOBScard. It's 17.9 cents per minute nationwide, any time of day. Like the NOBScard, there's no surcharge or application fee. You can ask for an application for the VoiceNet card from a dealer, such as Long Distance Telecom, at (800) 957-3494.

E-mail hook-up

In the past five years or so, E-mail has become the preferred method of communication for college students. Usually free, instantaneous, and extremely accessible, E-mail has made it possible for people to keep in touch with friends at other schools and at home like never before. Virtually every college or university will provide you with a free E-mail account for your four years at college. Most likely, your login name and passcode will be assigned to you randomly, and your account will be activated and ready for use by the time you arrive. If not, you'll have to fill out a form when you arrive at school, choosing a login name and a passcode; you may have to wait a few days for E-mail access.

P.O. box

Some schools provide students with a place to receive mail free of charge, but there is a possibility that you will have to rent a P.O. box for the year. The cost can range anywhere from $15 to $40. You'll be assigned a P.O. box number over the summer; if you're given the option, pay the fee then so your box can be activated. And give out the box number to family and friends before you leave for school. Along with requests for letters. Or money. You'll need it.

A bank account

Look for a national bank that has branches in your hometown; this will make your transactions a lot easier, especially when you go home over vacations or need your parents to transfer money into your account in an emergency. Also, many banks waive their monthly fee for six months for new customers. Look for these deals when choosing a bank, and pay attention to fees in general, especially per-check and per-ATM transaction fees. You'll probably want to get a basic checking account— you'll be writing a lot of checks in your first few weeks for installation fees, books, last-minute shopping for forgotten necessities, etcetera. (For more about finances, see chapter 6.)

Even more than getting settled in and choosing classes, Orientation Week is characterized by a flurry of introductions and whirlwind exchanges, as you repeatedly ask and are asked other freshmen's names, hometowns, high schools, and a number of other useless and quickly forgotten pieces of information. You'll meet most of these fellow first-years in your dorm, and while waiting on lines for various services. Chances are that more than once, you'll look for one of these familiar faces in the dining hall, and sit through an entire meal, all the while trying not to let on that you have forgotten your companion's name. Or you'll see someone you vaguely recognize on the street, and wonder whether you should smile and say hello or walk by while looking at the ground.

You may feel like an idiot, but *always* smile and say hello. During Orientation Week, it's doubtful that you will immediately, or even ever, bond with everyone you meet. But you never know. I met my current roommate during Orientation Week, otherwise known as "Camp Yale." And then there are people I can't believe I ever hung out with. But one of the great things about that first week is that anything goes; you're beginning with an entirely clean slate, and can build whatever types of friendships you choose. So take advantage of the opportunity. Go to events specifically for first-year students. Stay up until dawn talking to people you just met. Say hello to random people on the street. There's a social freedom you'll have during Orientation Week that you'll rarely experience again. Seize it.

ONLY THE LONELY

Despite the flurry of activity and the dozens of people you will meet during Orientation Week, before long you'll probably be missing your parents, your friends, your dog, maybe even your younger siblings. If you've never been on your own longer than six weeks during summer sleep-away camp, separation anxiety can rear its ugly head faster than Ebola. With everyone from far-off friends to anxious parents to long-distance loves miles away, it's easy to be surrounded by thousands of people and still feel completely alone. On the other hand, maybe the tables are turned, and you're fielding constant phone calls from your frantic parents, or trying to figure out how to drop your high school sweetheart like a bad habit in the least painful (for both of you) way possible. Whatever the case, you'll have a lot to deal with initially.

The 'Rents

Maybe your parents left for a second honeymoon after dropping you off. Maybe they converted your bedroom into a weight room. Maybe they had the phone company change their number to an unlisted one without informing you. If so, seek help elsewhere, for you have problems this book cannot address. More likely, your departure will produce a lot of strong (and maybe unexpected) feelings for both you and your parents. When it comes to your parents, reassure them that you miss them, that you'll stay in touch, that you have not become a deranged delinquent in their absence. The best thing you can do for them is let them know you're doing OK.

And when it comes to you, don't be afraid to call home once in a while if you're feeling especially lonely. Or better yet, E-mail if possible; it's free, it's fast, it's therapeutic, and you won't be spending hours on the phone wallowing in your misery.

FINDING YOUR FRIENDS ON THE INTERNET

Now that you have Internet access, you may be wondering what to do with it. One of the most enjoyable uses of the Internet is simply corresponding with people. If you know what college your friends go to, there's a good chance you can find out their E-mail addresses. Here are some tips:

- Try to navigate through his or her college's home page until you find a search function. You can get to a lot of colleges' home-pages through http://www.yahoo.com/regional/countries/united_states/education/colleges_and_universities/ or by searching for the college's name in Yahoo at http://www.yahoo.com/

- A guide at http://www.qucis.queensu.ca/faqs/email/college.html has instructions for how to find E-mail addresses of people from many different colleges. The guide deals with colleges alphabetically from Abilene Christian University to York University. This Web page also has links to several collections of college homepages.

- Though it may be a bit more difficult to use, a page at http://www.uiuc.edu/cgi-bin/ph/lookup might be helpful. When you call this page up, type the name of a college in the box labeled "Server" at the top of the screen. Then press ENTER. Then type the name of the person you're looking for. (If you can't find a particular college, you can get a list of all of the colleges that this page covers by following a link from their page entitled "all 326 CCSO Phonebook servers.")

- If you think your friend has a homepage, you can try typing his or her name into Altavista at http://altavista.digital.com (hint: put quotation marks around the name, as in "Joshua Davis"—this will help the searcher find the person you're looking for).

If homesickness for friends and families continues, try to do something constructive; talking for hours with your parents and going home every weekend is not going to alleviate any of the feelings that are prompting you to do those things. While you are keeping Kleenex and AT&T out of the red, other people are meeting each other, forging friendships, getting some action. So take a proactive approach—sample your campus' night life, join a club, take a lesson, talk to people. As hard as it might seem, it's the best cure for homesickness.

> Get out there, join some clubs, go Greek if you feel it's for you, and most of all take control of your life—*get involved* and you'll get the most out of your college experience.
>
> —Freshman, Virginia Polytechnic Institute and State University

The Long-Distance Relationship

A lot of freshmen arrive at college in September with more baggage than UPS can ship—a long-distance flame back home or at another school. Saying goodbye to a high school sweetheart can be one of the most painful aspects of leaving for college, and the temptation to spend hours on the phone with your long-distance love will no doubt be strong.

Obviously, no one can tell you what you should do about your long-distance relationship; you'll have to follow your instincts. Obsessing on your loneliness is not a good option, however, especially during your crucial first few weeks at college. As hard as it may seem, you'll be worse off in the long run if you can't wean yourself from the telephone or the computer, and make an effort to get out and meet people.

4 MEET YOUR ROOMIE

Is my roommate a psychopath? Will my roommate think that I am a psychopath? Am I a psychopath? These questions will plague you constantly in the weeks before you arrive on campus, even if, clinically speaking, you are entirely normal. Meeting your roommate(s) is at once the most stressful and exciting event of your first few days in college. When it comes to roommates, first impressions mean everything and they mean nothing; at your first meeting, you may believe you have found your soulmate or that you have made a mortal enemy. But chances are, the relationship will be a little more complicated and your feelings will be a little more ambivalent.

Freshmen often have high expectations when it comes to their roommate(s); they are expecting an instant best friend, a constant companion, someone (whew!) to eat with in the dining halls. And that actually may be kind of what it's like for the first few weeks. Soon, though, each of you will start to meet other people through classes, become involved with activities, and see each other progressively less. The good news is, if you hate each other, there are means of escape, there is life beyond your cubicle. Or maybe you'll miss the constant companionship. But the important thing to remember is that, as with any relationship, your relationship with your roommate will develop and change as you get to know each other, whatever your first impressions, and whatever the first few weeks are like.

So don't stress too much. This chapter aims to give you some tips on how to adjust to living with someone, particularly if it's a new experience for you, as well as provide you with the basics of roommate etiquette.

BEFORE THE MEETING: COMPLETING THE ROOMMATE QUESTIONNAIRE

You'll receive your roommate questionnaire at some point in the spring or early summer, after you've committed to a school and sent in your housing deposit. The real crapshoot, though, is getting matched with your roommate(s).

> From what I understand about how the residential life questionnaire works, schools pair up the people who say "I'm a relatively quiet person and I like to keep to myself" with the people who believe "College is a club with a $30,000 cover" in hopes that people, like numbers, average out when put together. Sometimes it works beautifully; I've seen roommates who go together better than Abbot and Costello. Other times, it's mixing matches and gasoline. Usually, it falls somewhere in between. Roommates tend to find the balance between tolerance and enjoyment.
>
> —Junior, Trinity College (Conn.)

The roommate portion of the questionnaire typically asks questions ranging from whether or not you smoke, to what hour you normally go to bed, to what type of music you listen to. You are also given the opportunity to make any special or specific requests about the type of person you want to live with.

Schools always honor certain requests, such as a preference for a nonsmoking roommate or a roommate who goes to bed early. Aside from those types of fundamental, lifestyle differences, however, there is no guarantee that other requests will be met.

Basically, when it comes to filling out the rooming questionnaire, there's not much you can do to guarantee compatibility, or even the sanity of your roommate. It's pretty much completely random—housing officers cheerfully play Russian roulette with your life. You should go into your situation with an open mind, though. Two roommates who meet freshman year might come from completely different backgrounds and have completely different tastes, and still go on to live together for four years. If, however, yours is not destined to be a love match, here's some roommate etiquette to guide you through the initial meeting, the honeymoon period, and the year.

THE MEETING

If you arrive at school first and know your roommate is also arriving the same day, don't be greedy. Don't be selfish. Don't sour the roommate relationship before it starts. In short, don't hog the nicest room, the nicest bed, the nicest closet, and the nicest dresser within milliseconds of your arrival. Waiting an hour to divide things up fairly is a "nice" gesture that will almost certainly be appreciated and will hopefully get your relationship off on the right foot.

When you and your roommate do finally meet, it's probably going to be awkward, especially if the parents are around, 'cause then you can't talk about them. Try not to bring up you boy/girlfriend from home, your boy/girlfriend down the hall, or your drug habit in the first five minutes of conversation. Intimate details of your personal life generally do not make for good getting-to-know-you chit-chat.

THE FIRST FEW DAYS

For the first week or so, you and your roommate(s) will be absorbed in furnishing and decorating your room. If you have to buy stuff, try not to split the cost of any items; rather, split up the items that need to be bought and purchase them separately. Haggling over money two days after you've met your roommate does not a happy friendship make. Besides, if you end up hating each other by the end of the year, the last thing you'll need is a bitter custody battle over a halogen lamp.

Dividing up your living space in the first couple of days probably won't lead to any great conflicts. Try to be fair; if you get the coveted bottom bunk, make some other concession to your roommate. But don't be a doormat either; allowing someone to walk all over you only breeds resentment, and resentment on either side can only make for bigger problems down the line.

FOR THE LONG HAUL:
GENERAL ROOMMATE ETIQUETTE

When the honeymoon period ends, keep the peace in your room by keeping the following things in mind:

- If it's important to your roommate, try to maintain a minimum standard of neatness, or at least hygiene. While no one should demand that you keep shared living space pristine and immaculate, can you really, in good conscience, force an innocent bystander to exist amidst your sloth? At the very least make a sincere effort; some people just can't be comfortable in a really messy room.

- Don't eat your roommate's food, borrow her clothes, or use shampoo without permission. Even if your roommate is annoyed by this, she might be hesitant to say so.

- Don't hog the phone. It's tempting to call family members, friends from home, and significant others often and for long periods of time, particularly in the first few weeks of school, but consider that you are effectively cutting your roommate off from civilization by doing so. So, call home when you feel lonely, of course, but remember that your roommate(s) may be feeling the same way, and take a stab at consideration. Besides, the trauma of weaning yourself from the telephone will be negligible compared to the pain when you receive the bill at the end of the month. Boy, do those long-distance charges add up.

- If you smoke or drink, and your roommate doesn't, be considerate; try to keep your vices out of the room. Smoking can cause physical irritation for a lot of people, so if your roommate objects, take the nicotine elsewhere.

- Don't blast music if you're roommate is studying. Seems fairly obvious, yet . . . .

- Remember to give your roommate messages. One person in our dorm freshman year was so upset by his roommate's forgetfulness that he hid the phone in his backpack. He literally carried it around with him for a whole day. It wasn't a cordless or a cell phone, so we never quite figured out what purpose his bizarre actions served. But he was obviously not a happy camper, and the episode culminated in a fistfight. The moral: Forget to pass on messages at your own risk.

- There are few things worse than being "sexiled" to the couch, or worse, to someone else's room.

Last year, my roommate's boyfriend from another school spent quite a bit of time with us. He was visiting the night before my bio midterm and the night before my bio final. But I figured, it gave my roommate peace of mind—she said she wanted to marry this guy. So this year what does she do? She breaks up with him for a Columbia guy. So I put up with all that for a doomed relationship. I was so mad at her when I heard.

—Sophomore, Columbia University

If you don't have single, but you have a significant other staying the night, or are otherwise in need of bedroom privacy, do not automatically assume that your roommate will be accommodating. Often, you can strike a deal with you roommate, as in, "Next weekend you do couch duty," but sometimes it's not that simple. As (literally) painful as it might be, ultimately, you have to respect your roommate's wishes. But everybody goes out of town sooner or later . . . .

THE LIGHTER SIDE OF ROOMMATE RELATIONSHIPS

If you think your roommate is crazy, just remember that things could always get worse. Has he or she ever tried any of these stunts? (Excerpted from the popular Internet item "50 Ways to Confuse Your Roommate")

- Steal a fishtank. Fill it with beer and dump sardines in it. Talk to them.

- Spend all your money on transformers. Play with them at night. If your roommate says anything, tell him with a straight face, "They're more than meets the eye."

- Chain yourself to your roommate's bed. Get her to bring you food.

- Get a computer. Leave it on when you are not using it. Turn it off when you are.

- Ask your roommate if your family can move in "just for a couple of weeks."
- Fake a heart attack. When your roommate gets the paramedics to come, pretend nothing happened.
- Smile. All the time.
- Burn all your waste paper while eying your roommate suspiciously.
- Always flush the toilet three times.
- Give him an allowance.
- Listen to radio static.

Chances are, sometimes you'll find yourself on the receiving end of breaches of roommate etiquette. As reluctant as you might be to do so, it's perfectly within your rights to speak up. Your roommate may just not realize that he is being inconsiderate, and in all likelihood it will only take a complaint (or two) to improve the situation. Communication is key. If your roommate is doing something that makes you want to blanket her with paper cuts and lemon juice, say something. Be direct but tactful—usually, "The music was a little loud last night," is more effective that "You are a lunatic and I wish you didn't have a key to my room." Similarly, really listen and respond to what your roommate says to you.

If the lines of communication fail and speaking up doesn't work, just hire a hit man . . . oh wait, we're getting ahead of ourselves. If speaking up doesn't work, there's bound to be resentment, and when there's resentment, there's conflict.

Having lived in a freshman residence hall three years now, I've seen roommates who keep their frustrations in, not willing to say anything, hoping that it goes away. But usually doesn't. Instead, it festers, it eats away at them. They begin to snap at each other for the littlest things. "You moved my stuff," he yells, while he means "You drink in the residence with your friends all night long, all week long, and it's gotten to the point where I no longer feel comfortable in my own room."

And then one day it blows up. One roommate or the other calls up his R.A. and says "I can't live with that person anymore." And in spite of all efforts to reconcile roommate issues, it is impossible. What once were little scratches have become much larger wounds.

In the long run, it's best to talk things out with your roommate from the beginning.

—Junior, Trinity College (Conn.)

CONFLICT RESOLUTION

You have tried everything. You've discussed a problem politely with your roommate. You've yelled. You've slammed doors. You've played hardball, dividing the room in half with masking tape. Everything has failed. It's time to seek outside help.

Whatever you do, do not begin by discussing roommate problems with other friends. The rumor mill in a dorm is a real marvel, a true phenomenon; gossip spreads at warp speed and infects every floor like the plague. So, even though it's tempting to tell friends that your roommate is a freak, resist—your words will someday (soon) come back to haunt you, guaranteed.

Instead, you might want begin by talking to a Resident Assistant (R.A.), or Freshman Counselor, usually a senior who lives in the freshman dorms and advises a group of students. A dean of student affairs (usually there is a specific administrator assigned to each dorm) might also be helpful. These counselors can try to help you resolve your conflicts with your roommate, or at least help you identify alternatives to homicide.

If all else fails, though, if it becomes clear that you and your roommate are fundamentally incompatible, you can request to be moved to another room. If you find that conflicts with your roommate are interfering with your academic work, your self-esteem, or your peace of mind, it's time to get out of that situation. Talk to your freshman counselor, your college dean, or some other advisor and let them know that the situation has become intolerable. Most colleges have singles set aside for such circumstances.

Meeting your roommate is probably one of your most anticipated aspects of college life. You shouldn't begin your year with either the expectation that you will hate your roommate or the certainty that you will be best friends—the overwhelming majority of freshman rooms fall somewhere in the middle. Go into the situation with an open mind, and no matter what, keep the lines of communication open from the beginning.

Dorm Life

If you're like most freshmen, you'll be spending your first year living in the dorms, sharing a small, spartan cubicle—let's call it a "room," for argument's sake—with one or several strangers. For at least your first year, and probably all of your college experience, your dorm will serve as the nexus of your life, the place where you study, sleep, and socialize, where you'll find friendship, romance, and vermin.

Most colleges require students to live on campus in one of the dorms for their first or first two years. Even if your school allows the option of finding an off-campus apartment as a freshman, it's a good idea to live in the dorms for at least a year, if you can afford it. Freshman year, the dorms jumpstart your social life, ease the transition to life on your own, and force you to learn how to play well with others. Sure, living in a dorm has its drawbacks, but most people find that the rewards outweigh the frustrations—you trade privacy for constant companionship, and convenience for independence.

Diversity University

You might not be prepared for the enormous diversity you'll encounter among your dormmates at most schools. For a lot of students, living in the dorms freshman year is their first opportunity to meet people from different parts of the country and the world, people of different religions, races, economic backgrounds, or sexual orientations. This is good. This is life. It's a very particular type of preparation for the real world; in the real world, people meet, work with, argue with, and fall in love with all different kinds. So try to approach everything and everyone with an open mind, with respect, and with honesty. What you'll learn from this particular dose of the real world and this interaction with very different kinds of people will be just as valuable as what you learn in your classes.

YOUR FRIENDLY NEIGHBORHOOD R.A.

Your Resident Assistant (R.A.) is an upperclassman (usually a junior or a senior) selected by your school to live in your dorm and act as your counselor/advisor/tutor/mentor/mediator/friend. Sometimes an R.A. is assigned to each floor or wing in a dorm. During your first weeks, if you're feeling lonely, stressed, or tempted to poison your roommate, your R.A. can be a sympathetic and helpful listener. He can also be an indispensable academic resources, giving you advice on courses, professors, and choosing a major. Finally, your R.A. can also help mediate disputes between you and your roommate or dormmate, curbing disagreements before they snowball into intractable problems. Remember: Your R.A. is also charged with the responsibility of enforcing dorm rules, so don't offer him a beer to help you celebrate your eighteenth birthday.

TYPES OF DORMS

When you get your rooming questionnaire over the summer, you may be asked if you want to live in a special dorm. In addition, some schools may give you the option of living on a special floor, like an all-female floor or a chemical-free floor, within a standard dorm. Different schools have different options, but these are some of the most common:

Single-sex dorms

If you've been awaiting the opportunity to live in close quarters with members of the opposite sex since you were twelve, read no further. If, however, you don't feel comfortable in a coed dorm, many schools have all-female or (less commonly) all-male facilities. Beware, though: These types of dorms sometimes have restrictions concerning guests of the opposite sex, overnight or otherwise.

A coed dorm is the only setting where you can get to know people of the opposite sex really well and maintain close friendships with them—people in the hallway are pretty tight. The other thing is, there are a lot of hallway hookups. But the problem is, when you hook up with someone from the hallway, you don't know how to act afterwards, if you don't want it to be a real relationship.

—Junior, Cornell University

Chemical- or substance-free dorms

These dorms prohibit smoking, drinking, and drugs. If you avoid alcohol or other substances because of personal, moral, or religious reasons, this might be an option for you. You can also worry less about kegs in the bathroom and vomit in the hallway if you choose to live in one of these dorms.

Quiet dorms

These dorms restrict the noise level between certain hours, or, in some cases, 24 hours a day. Obviously, the quiet dorm in not the social hub of campus, but if you really need your uninterrupted study time and sleep time, this might be right for you.

Special-interest or "theme" housing

Some schools offer the option of living in a "theme" house; for instance, there might be a dorm for students who speak Spanish, or are premed, or are international students. The good part, of course, is that you'll meet students with whom you share interests. On the flip side, though, this means you might miss out on meeting a more diverse group of people, one of the best aspects of and opportunities afforded by living on campus.

In our arts theme house, we have a rush process and basically encourage artists to rush. It's much tamer than Greek rush—there's no hazing, there's no pledging, and it's really low-key. I wanted to live here because it would be a community that would support my efforts and complement them. I hoped that it would give me more opportunities to perform, and it has.

—Sophomore, Duke University

TYPES OF ROOMS

Some schools also give you the option of choosing what kind of room you want to live in, although this is more often assigned randomly. In most cases, you'll be living in either a room off of a hallway, or a suite with one or more bedrooms and a living room. You'll also probably be sharing a bathroom with many other people on your floor or hallway, which means morning races for the shower and long treks to brush your teeth. Some schools have separate bathrooms for men and women, but it's possible you'll be sharing your shower (figuratively speaking, of course) with members of the opposite sex.

Singles

At most schools, it's pretty rare to get a single as a freshman. Having a single has its obvious perks, but there are some negatives, too. You don't get a roommate, a.k.a. instant companion, to share your first few weeks (and expenses) with.

> Living in a single as a freshman was tough for the first two weeks at school. Since some of my sophomore hallmates already had established groups of friends, finding my own group of friends was a little tough. I did finally find good friends to hang out with, but they lived in a dorm across the street. Now, I find living in a single a blessing. I still go across the street to hang out, but when I really need to study, I have the peace and quiet of a room of my own. Even though I will live with my friends next year, living in a single as a freshman has been a positive experience.
>
> —Freshman, University of Michigan (Ann Arbor)

Doubles

A double, which means you share a bedroom with one other person, is by far the most common setup at most schools. The size of your bedroom will probably necessitate bunked beds and make for very little privacy.

Triples

One-bedroom triples are pretty rare, but it's been known to happen at schools with housing shortages. This is not a good arrangement; not only is it crowded, but triples tend to fall into a certain formula: two roommates bond like a tongue to a flagpole in December, while the third ends up feeling left out in the cold.

Suites

Not too many schools offer this option to freshman, but it's a nice one. Usually, these suites consist of a couple of bedrooms and some kind of shared living space. For instance, a quad (four people) might be made up of two double bedrooms and one common room. You get the best of both world with this option; you can go into your bedroom to sleep or whatever, while your roommate studies or talks on the phone in the common room.

There will probably be several rooms or suites on your floor and several floors on your dorms. Generally, dorms have some amenities; yours probably will have a laundry room with coin-operated washers and dryers, as well as student lounges on every floor. Some schools have other spaces and facilities you share with your dormmates, like kitchens, study areas, or TV rooms. Freshman year, these spaces are constantly occupied; you always know you can find students discussing the meaning of life in the lounge or fighting over the remote in the TV room. This is one of the most fun and comforting parts of dorm life, especially freshman year. People drift in and out of common spaces constantly, so there's rarely a shortage of people to talk to or share a late-night pizza with.

Depending on how many people live on your floor or in your dorm, dormmates often bond like crazy. Sharing space 24 hours a day with people means you drift in and out of each other's rooms, borrow clothes and CDs from each other, get to know about each other's families, relationships, and aspirations. Be warned, though: Gossip spreads through dorms faster than mono. You tell your roommate something about someone else "confidentially," and he "confidentially" tells your next-door neighbor, and she tells her roommate, who puts it on her homepage, and, well, you get the picture.

BEAUTIFY YOUR PAD: DECORATION AND STORAGE

Storage space in the typical dorm room is extremely limited, which means you're going to have to get creative to keep your room from looking like it should be condemned. Plastic stackable crates are really useful; you can lug your belongings from home in them, and then use them to store your stuff. Or stack them upside down to use as a makeshift table or nightstand. They don't take up much room, they fit just about anywhere, and you can find them in sets of three for less than $10. Underbed storage bins or shelf units can also help you organize your space.

No matter how creative you get, though, chances are you'll have to accept that you can't bring everything you've ever owned with you to college. What was the mantra? Less is more, less is more . . . .

One area in which you shouldn't skimp, however, is in decorating your new home. A comfortable and personalized living space can do wonders for your stress level; even it's not a posh and padded house of opulence, you should at least look forward to coming home to it. Again, find out what your roommates can bring, and get their take on how they want to decorate the room. You don't want to make any major interior decorating decisions without their consent, or at least knowledge. Your roommates might not be pleased when they arrive to find your room a rhapsody in pink and baby blue, complete with lace curtains and your stuffed animal collection. Realize you may have to compromise when it comes to decorating; your room will probably end up being a schizophrenic mix of your respective tastes.

> Posters are a must, and remember to tell your roommates that van Gogh is not the only artist that has produced good works. I think if I had a penny for every *Starry Night* I see in our hall, I would have enough change to do my weekly laundry.
>
> —Freshman, Harvard University

Decorating a room with limited space and a limited budget usually turns into a genuine challenge. Art prints and movie posters are a common stand-by, and college students are at last progressing beyond the swarm of Monet prints and *Pulp Fiction* posters that have invaded dorm rooms across the country over the last few years. Hanging tapestries on the wall can also give your room a little personality (although some schools also consider these a fire hazard, for some incomprehensible reason). And some schools let students paint their rooms, as long as they paint them back to their original color (probably "eggshell white") at the end of the year. If you're ambitious, this can be a fun (but expensive), project. But probably the most important thing to remember are pictures of family, a stuffed animal, or other reminders of home; these personal touches are really the only things that will make your room feel like home.

BASIC DORM-ROOM HYGIENE

If the last time you held a broom was your third-grade Halloween party and you have never done a load of laundry in your life, you may be in for a shock when you arrive at college.

Mom doesn't live here anymore.

You can probably get away with living in whatever level of squalor you wish, as long as your roommate agrees, and you're not fined by the fire marshal for excess debris (it's been known to happen). If you are at all inclined to live in generally sanitary or hygienic conditions, however, bring some cleaning supplies from home, especially if you have your own bathroom. Cleaning fluids and items like a mop, a broom, and a dustpan are indispensable throughout the year, and especially when you arrive on campus. Rooms accumulate a lot of dust during the summer, and may not be in the best shape when you make your entrance.

If you're really disciplined, you can try creating some kind of cleanup schedule with your roommates, but you'd probably be better off just keeping your own stuff off the floor and out of each other's paths and discarding rotting food at regular intervals. Here are a couple of handy-dandy tips for keeping your room (at least on the surface) spic and span:

Get dark-colored rugs and furniture.
The beer stains blend right in.

Buy stackable storage bins like they're going out of style.
They're inexpensive, fit discreetly in the corner, and help keep your crap off the floor.

Get a recycling bin if your school didn't issue you one.
Too many old newspapers and magazines make your room look like you're trying to housebreak a puppy.

Throw away your Twinkie wrappers and pizza boxes.
Take out your trash regularly, especially if it contains old food containers (or worse, old food). That stuff not only can leave your room smelling like a pit as well as looking like one, but it can also attract vermin previously seen only in low-budget horror movies.

If you do end up with roaches, ants, or spiders, invest in some industrial-strength Raid pronto.
Spray only in well-ventilated areas and don't spray into the air. You can sicken an entire apartment full of people if you don't respect the power of Raid. If your insect problem becomes unmanageable, or if you spot little Mickey mice or (God help you) rats, it's time to call in the big guns. Tell your R.A. about the problem, and she should be able to provide you with some traps or tell you where to go from there.

Keep your room well-stocked with ashtrays if you plan to let people smoke in it.
Cigarette burns are impossible to fix and hard to hide, especially if they're in the middle of your beautiful rug. Also, keep your windows open so your room doesn't smell like smoke for days afterward.

Keep a bottle of seltzer at arm's length.
It'll be helpful in removing alcohol, vomit, or blood stains.

Overcoming Laundry Room Anxiety

> Most people, especially the guys, wait until their underwear runs out before they finally break down and do laundry.
>
> —Junior, Cornell University

If you can't keep your dorm room clean, at least try for your underwear. Again, Mom doesn't live here anymore, and if she's washed and ironed your clothes for you all your life, you may arrive at college a scared and skittish laundry virgin. Have no fear, though; it's not as difficult as it seems, and after a few shrunken shirts and pink socks, you'll be doing your occasional load like a pro.

Most dorms have laundry rooms with coin-operated washers and dryers in their basements. The University of Pennsylvania recently began a system whereby students can do their laundry for free, but the vast majority of you will not be so lucky. So take a trip to the bank and stack up on quarters before you arrive at school, because you may not find a change machine when you get there.

Available washers and dryers are usually a scarce commodity. You'll have the most trouble finding free machines on weekends and in the evenings. If you have a big chunk of time one day during the week, you might want to beat the rush. Arrive armed with your laundry bag, enough quarters for all your loads, detergent, fabric softener, and a sawed-off shotgun.

Adventures in Laundry and Ironing

How many laundry commercial catch phrases can you identify?

- Before you head down to the laundry room, use a stain-remover to pretreat any clothing with hard-to-remove stains.

- Pay attention to the labels on your clothes. If they're in another language, get someone to translate. You should be able to hunt down someone who speaks Urdu in your dorm. After all, "Dry-Clean Only" is not a phrase you want to miss.

- Always, always separate whites and colors to prevent bleeding, unless you want your laundry to look like something out of a bad Tide™ commercial. You should also separate towels, pillowcases, or other linens from the rest of your wash; they tend to be bleeders, too.

- Never overload; this goes for both washers and dryers. Your laundry never gets clean enough or dry enough, and it's not worth the three quarters you might save yourself.

- Use a detergent with color-safe bleach. It whitens whites and brightens colors! (And read the directions before you empty the entire bottle into the washing machine.)

- Don't forget the fabric softener. Unless you like the silky feel of sandpaper on your skin, taking a second to throw a sheet of fabric softener in the dryer is a must when it comes to your towels and clothes.

- The laundry room can be a dangerous place. Someone could be silently stalking you, just waiting for you turn your back or leave the room so he can make your Levi's disappear into the Bermuda Triangle. If you can't sit there and guard your clothes like a German shepherd, watch the time carefully so you know when to come back. You'll avoid finding your clothes in a heap on the ground, or worse, having them stolen by some covetous laundry room looter.

- Fold your clothes right after you take them out of the dryer. If you fold them quickly enough and just the right way, you might be able to spare yourself the unpleasant task of ironing.

- If you do, in fact, have to iron, try to use one of those mini-ironing boards. Or try ironing on top of a folded towel.

- Before you start, spray cotton clothes lightly with water, and check to make sure your iron's clean.

Dorm life, like everything, has its drawbacks and its rewards, but most people enjoy the big, noisy, family-like atmosphere of the dorms. Even if you have the opportunity to live off campus as a freshman, give the dorms a try; from same-dorm romantic relationships, to constant companionship, to accessible social functions, dorm life offers a lot of intangibles that are especially valuable freshman year.

6 Money Management

No sooner do you settle into your dorm room than responsibility comes pounding at your door. And responsibility brings friends. The bursar, the financial aid office, the bank, your credit card company, and even Uncle Sam are trying to get in on the act. If it's the first time you've really had to handle your own finances, juggling it all can seem a daunting task.

Whether you find a campus job to meet expenses or your parents feed your account, managing it—and keeping yourself in the black—is entirely your responsibility. And in a world of plastic, your credit cards(s) and ATM card can appear dangerously like an unlimited supply of cash, like a shining beacon that lights your path to spending nirvana, when in reality it lures you into the economic abyss. Managing an account and your credit cards conservatively and still having enough cash for books, beer, and the occasional tattoo is a task that requires skill and patience.

Hidden Expenses
As if $25,000 weren't enough.

In addition to tuition, fees, and room and board costs, prepare yourself for an onslaught of hidden fees when you arrive on campus. Chances are, you'll have to pay up to $200 for phone installation (i.e., flipping a switch) and service, room connection fees for Internet service, and a post office box rental fee.

I was surprised by how much money I had to spend even before school started. Books, stuff for my room, and everything else—it just added all up. My checking account went all the way down to nothing, and I actually bounced a check by accident. Of course it was an accident. Luckily, I was only about 30 minutes away from home, so I was never in danger of being stranded without any money.

—Senior, California Polytechnic University at Pomona

Then there are the academic costs. Expect to spend between $200–$500 on textbooks and course packets per semester, depending on your subjects. You can try to save money on books by hunting down used texts, which can cost a fraction of the price of brand-new textbooks. Some campus bookstores buy back used books from students and resell them at lower prices the following year. You can also search for used book shops, take advantage of student book agencies, or find upperclassmen who are willing to give or sell their books to you. These students often advertise in school publications or post ads around campus.

Other academic costs may include a small fortune in materials fees for any art or photography classes you might be taking. Also, if you don't have your own printer, you'll have to factor the cost of laser printing cards into your budget.

In addition to utilities and academic costs, basic living costs can leave a mighty big dent in your wallet. Sooner or later (probably later), you're going to run out of fabric softener. Sooner or later (probably sooner), you're going to get a midnight craving for pizza. The point is, you'll have a lot more personal expenses and need a lot more cash than you bargained for, and you'll need someplace bigger than your piggy bank to keep it in.

BANKING

To set up your bank account, you'll need to present at least two forms of photo identification (leave your fake ID at home) and your social security card. Most banks require that students be 18 years old to open an account, so if you have a late birthday and will be only 17 when school starts, open your account while your parents are still around.

When you do set up your account, you have a couple of different options to chooses from:

Savings accounts
The major benefit to getting a savings account is that you receive interest on your money, although the rate may be negligible (between 1 and 2 percent). Often, you also receive an ATM (automated teller machine) card with your savings account that lets you to make a certain number of withdrawals each month. If you have an account with ATM privileges at home, there's probably no reason to open up a savings account at school. You'll probably be better off getting a checking account, which is what the vast majority of college students end up with.

Money market account
Money market accounts are basically glorified savings accounts—you get a fairly high level of interest if you keep a fairly high minimum balance in your account. If your balance dips below the minimum, you get charged a hefty fine. You'll probably get only three checks per month with these types of accounts, and if you write more, guess what? You also get a hefty fine. These accounts are probably not ideal for most college students, who often need to write a lot of checks to cover things like rent, phone bills, and utility bills.

Checking accounts
Checking accounts are useful because they let you avoid carrying cash; in-state checks are widely accepted forms of payment (as long as you produce a photo ID), and canceled checks serve as irrefutable proof of purchase. Your bank will also issue you the all-important ATM card when you open up a checking account. Typically, you don't receive interest on money in a regular checking account; if your bank does offer some paltry rate, you may have to maintain an impossibly high minimum balance. Most checking accounts allow you unlimited checks and ATM withdrawals. NOW (Negotiable Order of Withdrawal) accounts are checking accounts that pay interest; the amount of checks or ATM withdrawals is typically limited, and if you exceed the stated amount, or if your balance dips below the minimum, your bank might assess a fine.

What to Look For

Someone who's intelligent, attractive, and sensitive, who really listens to what you have to say . . . oh. What to look for in a bank. Well, when choosing a bank or an account type, try to find out the following information:

What are the monthly fees?

Monthly fees vary widely between banks and among accounts. Some banks don't charge monthly fees for the first six months or year after you open an account; don't automatically accept one of these offers before finding out what the regular fees are. Compare among banks to find the lowest possible fee, because after a while, the monthly charges really add up.

Is there a minimum balance?

Some banks require you to keep a certain amount of money in your account, and levy hefty penalties and fees if you dip below that amount. Look for an account with no minimum balance.

Are there limited transactions?

Some banks allow you to write a certain number of checks or make a certain number of ATM withdrawals in a month. If you exceed that maximum, the bank may assess a per-check or per-ATM transaction fee.

Does your bank charge for foreign ATMs?

In other words, is there a fee, and how much is it, if you use your ATM card at a bank other than your own?

If you do decide to get a checking account, and have never managed your own before, there are a few things you need to remember, both to protect yourself and to keep yourself in good standing with the bank. The most important thing is to keep a record of any checks that you write (and any ATM transactions that you make).

Also remember to save any deposit receipts. You can deposit money in your account either in person at your bank, or through your bank's ATM machine at any time. Either way, make sure you get and keep a record of the transaction; you'll need it when it comes time to balance the ol' checkbook. Find out from your bank how long it takes for a deposited check to clear; it's usually about three days, but the time can vary between one and seven days. Don't write a check if you're not positive your deposits have cleared and you have enough money in the account to cover it.

Bouncing a check is not only embarrassing, it can cause significant damage to your credit rating and (surprise!) draw a hefty fine (maybe more than the amount of the check) from your bank. Few banks offer overdraft protection on student accounts, so it's up to you to always make sure you keep track of how many checks you've written, and above all, how many ATM withdrawals you've made. You can call your bank or get an ATM balance statement at any time to find out what your balance is. If your checkbook is lost or stolen, you should not be held responsible for any forged checks that clear; it's the bank's responsibility to make sure the signature on each of your checks is yours, by comparing them to a copy of your signature that they keep on file. To save yourself and everyone else a lot of hassle, though, report a lost or stolen checkbook to your bank right away.

If you lose an actual check that you've written, you can contact your bank and request that they issue a stop payment, which will prevent any idiot off the street from coming in and trying to cash it. Banks can charge up to $15 for this service, but it's worth the peace of mind.

The ATM

The problem with ATM machines is that you take out money in $20 denominations. And if I take out $20 to buy, say, a mocha, my tendency is to spend the rest of it as quickly as possible. Unfortunately, I buy a lot of mochas. And that's a lot of $20 bills. So I find myself going to the ATM more and more frequently, and watching the money in my account slowly dwindle by small increments.

—Senior, Yale University

Who says money doesn't grow on trees? Nowadays, you can get free and unlimited cash at any number of conveniently located, 24-hour Always Tons of Money machines.

Ok, maybe not. Unfortunately, that's what it feels like. It's all too easy to make withdrawal after withdrawal at the many cash machines that may line your campus more densely than trees. But $20 here and $20 there can add up incredibly fast, and before you know it you've sucked your account completely dry, or even bounced a check or two. Bank cards have become the single easiest way to access your money, but their very convenience can make you feel like a (rich) kid in a candy store. Here are some fundamental ATM commandments to keep yourself out of the red:

- Come up with a four- to six-digit PIN (personal identification number) that's easy for you to remember but hard for somebody else to figure out. Your birthday, for example, is not a good choice (especially if your ATM card inhabits the same wallet as your driver's license.) Keep your PIN number written down somewhere safe—not in your purse or wallet—just in case you forget it. And, never, ever tell your PIN number to anyone else.

- Keep all of your ATM withdrawal receipts so you can check them against your account statements at the end of the month. They're also a reminder of how fast you're going through your cash.

- Consciously limit your withdrawals. Unusual and unexpected expenses come up, of course, but you can try limiting your withdrawals to a certain figure each week. Otherwise, you might find yourself taking out $20—you generally withdraw ATM funds in multiples of $20—every time you "need" some small item, and then blowing the change.

- Avoid "foreign" ATMs as often as possible. Banks can charge anywhere from 50 cents to $1.50 for each ATM transaction you make at cash machines operated by other banks. It doesn't sound like much, but when you're making a couple of transactions a week, the charges start to add up.

- If you lose your card, contact the bank as soon as you notice. There's little danger that anyone will actually be able to withdraw money from your account, but reporting the loss or theft immediately will keep you protected. Also, you'll want your replacement right away, and it can take a week or two from the time you call your bank for your new cash card to arrive in your mailbox.

PLASTIC, PLASTIC, EVERYWHERE

When the need for textbooks and the desire for CDs strike, "Charge" remains the battle cry of college students everywhere. If you don't already have your own credit card by the time you arrive at school, your opportunity to tumble into debt will come soon enough.

Swarms of credit card companies will stuff your mailbox with offers especially for students. Representatives from banks and companies will stalk you on the street outside the bookstore, with offerings of "pre-approved" charge cards and complimentary plastic mugs. It can be very easy—maybe too easy—for college students to qualify for credit, even if they have never previously used a credit card and have no income. Credit card companies usually don't even run background checks on students, requiring only a student ID, a social security number, and a phone number to sign up.

It's probably a good idea to get a credit card right away if you don't already have one; they're good to have, even if only for emergencies, and are a fast way to build a good credit rating. Unfortunately, they can also be a fast way to build a bad credit rating. Using a credit card responsibly is absolutely vital when you're a student, especially if your parents aren't footing the bills and you have no steady income. So before you sell your soul to Visa™, investigate your options.

Types of Cards

There are three basic types of cards: credit, charge, and debit.

Credit cards

A credit card is the most common kind of plastic students carry. They're issued by credit card corporations or banks, and the most widely accepted ones are Visa™, Mastercard™, and Discover™. Generally with these cards, you have to pay only a percentage of your bill or a small, fixed minimum payment each month. If you pay only the minimum, get ready to fork over a hefty finance charge on top of your balance next month. Some credit cards also double as phone cards, which let you make long-distance phone calls from anywhere.

Charge cards

Charge cards such as American Express™ generally have no spending limit, but require that you pay your balance in full each month, or be subject to dizzying fees. These cards force you to spend within your means and keep you from carrying over debt from month to month. Missing a payment, though, is murder on both your credit rating and your wallet, and the company will not hesitate to cancel your charging privileges. Dining and entertainment cards are essentially charge cards as well, and department stores frequently offer charge cards for exclusive use in their stores.

Debit cards

Debit cards, unlike credit or charge cards, don't involve loans or interest. When you use a debit card to make a purchase at the store, the amount is deducted from your bank account, like a check. Some banks issue ATM cards that you can use as debit cards, like checks, at stores that have the facilities to process them. If your bank has per-check or foreign ATM fees, it may charge for this service.

Bring on the Plastic

When you're shopping for a card, look for a bank or corporation that is widely (preferably internationally) accepted and well established. Even if you find a card with low interest rates and no annual fee, it won't do you much good if no one accepts it for purchases. Also, more established banks and companies offer crucial services, like 24-hour hotlines to report lost or stolen cards, or insurance for valuable purchases made on the card.

As you sift through the credit options that pour into your mailbox and assault you on street corners, there are a few terms you should know:

Annual fee

Some banks require that you pay an automatic yearly fee. Many banks and credit corporations waive the annual fee for college students for their first year, or for as long as they're full-time students. Shop around for a card with no annual fee, and find out whether the offer is just a "teaser" that won't continue the following year.

Credit line

Banks and credit corporations usually offer credit lines of $500–$600 to first-time cardholders. If you make payments responsibly and on time, the bank or company will automatically extend your credit line at regular intervals. If you have some sort of emergency, you can try calling the lender; they may be able to extend your credit line slightly on request.

Finance charges

Some banks stick you with automatic finance charges every month; others extort, I mean, assess, charges for late payments or failure to meet the minimum payment.

Percent APR

Percent APR is the percent interest per year that you pay on all purchases you make with your card. Fixed APRs typically range from 16 to 20 percent, and some places give you a lower teaser rate that goes up in following year. Some APRs are variable, which means they shift with each billing period on the basis of outside factors, usually the prime rate reported by the *Wall Street Journal* plus a fixed amount of percentage points.

Grace period

A grace period is the time you have to pay off balances on your purchases without shelling out interest. In other words, if you pay your bill in full before the 25–30 day grace period is up, you don't have to pay any interest at all on those purchases.

Now that you're on your own, you might want a credit card (or two, three, or four) to assert your independence. Here are a few standard—and one not-so-standard—cards to get. All have no application fee or annual fees:

- *AT&T Universal Mastercard:* Apply online at http://www.att. com/ucs/college/col_menu.html or call customer service at (800) 423-4343.

- *Star Trek Mastercard:* It's a great conversation starter and, if you're interested in *Star Trek,* definitely worthwhile. Apply online at http://www.webapply.com/startrek/ or call (800) WEB-APPLY.

- *Discover:* Offers insignificant cash-back bonus awards that still may be nice to get. Hey, it's free! Call (800) DISCOVER for more information.

- *Citibank Visa:* You can print out an application from the online site at http://www.citibank.com/us/cards/cgi-bin/chooser.cgi, but you will have to print out the form and mail it in. Citibank's customer service number is (800) 950-5114.

- *American Express:* The Optima™ card has no annual fee. Apply online at http://www.americanexpress.com/student/thecards/ thecards.html or call (800) 942-2639.

Using Your Credit Card Wisely

Credit card purchases are even harder to keep track of than ATM withdrawals, especially now that so many places, from the post office to that liquor store that doesn't card, accept them. Here are some hints for wielding your plastic wisely:

- Keep all receipts of credit card purchases. You'll want to check your monthly statement against them for accuracy. And while you're keeping track of your purchases, try setting spending limits for yourself that you refuse to exceed, no matter what.

- Try to pay off your balance in full in each month. If you can't do that, send as much as you can afford. If you get into the habit of making only the minimum payments, you'll be hit with finance charges from hell.

- If it's a struggle to pay off your balance in full in more than a couple of cycles, put the card away. It's way too easy to spend now and worry about the consequences later. Groveling to your parents can be a humbling experience, so think about that before you spend hundreds on sex toys.

- Don't get cash advances—whereby you use your credit card to withdraw money from an ATM—on one card to pay off your balance on another. In fact, avoid cash advances whenever you can help it; there's no grace period for them, which means interest begins accruing immediately.

A Final Word on Credit Cards

If your parents offer to put you on their credit card, take them up on it. Of course, you might want to let them know before making purchases, and we wouldn't recommend charging items like your new Rollerblades to their Visa card. But you may need their higher spending limit in case of a medical emergency, or to buy a plane ticket home for Thanksgiving break. You'll probably still want to get your own card for personal expenses, but keeping one of theirs for emergencies is something you should definitely consider.

ACADEMIC UTOPIA

part 2

CHOOSING YOUR COURSES

You've decided that you want voice mail instead of an answering machine, what your E-mail passcode will be, and where to do your banking. Now it's time for some real choices: what are you taking this semester? Many schools have you choose classes during orientation week, others require you to preregister over the summer, and still others, like Yale and Bucknell, have a one- to two-week "shopping period" at the beginning of the semester, during which you can sample various lectures and sections, get a feel for different professors, and hunt down smaller classes.

Most schools require you to preregister, and this registration usually takes one of two forms: easy, modern phone registration, and inconvenient, archaic in-person hassle. If your school still subscribes to the latter method, arrive at registration early, or you might get shut out of classes you want.

> There was one class that was so popular, it was absolutely impossible to get in. I went there an hour early to sign up, thinking that an hour would be enough time to secure a spot. But by the time I got there, there were so many people, I couldn't believe it! Some people had been waiting there for over 3 hours, playing cards and doing homework. I tried to find the end of the line, only to find myself on the fifth floor of the building. (The line started on the first floor.) I'm planning to take the class next year, and I'll definitely remember to get to the class at least two hours ahead.
>
> —Sophomore, Yale University

Whenever you register, you'll need the scoop on different academic calendars and credit systems, and some general guidelines for choosing courses and figuring out your first-semester schedule.

THE ACADEMIC CALENDAR

The academic calendar and credit system, which will determine how many courses you take in how long a period, as well as your vacation and exam schedule, varies from school to school. The following are the most common systems:

The semester system
Most schools work on a semester system, dividing the year into two terms. Students are generally expected to carry an average of 15 credit hours per semester; that means four courses each semester if each course carries four credit hours, and five if your school works on a three-credit system. If you're taking a science course that requires extra hours in the laboratory, you can probably expect to receive anywhere from one to two additional credits.

The trimester system
Some schools, such as the University of Chicago and Stanford University, operate on a trimester system, which usually means three ten-week quarters—fall, winter, and spring. Typically, students at these colleges take an average of three courses per quarter. Freshmen who attend schools on trimester systems often complain that their academic schedules and vacation weeks rarely coincide with those of their friends from home. Also, with three shorter academic terms, it can seem like your life constantly revolves around studying for midterm exams, and, just when the caffeine from midterms has left your system, studying for finals. On the plus side, taking only three courses per term allows you delve into material more intensively, and gives you a fighting chance at doing all your reading for all your classes before exam week arrives.

The four-one-four calendar
At some schools, such as Middlebury College, students take four courses in the fall, four courses in the spring, and one in-depth course or independent research project in January, known as a J-term. There are numerous variations on this system, but all are intended to provide you

with one intensive, nontraditional classroom experience. The value of J-terms varies by school and by student; one student's month of in-depth research might be another's extended vacation.

PLANNING YOUR SEMESTER: THE BASICS

Whatever your school's academic calendar, you face what at first seems a daunting task when it comes time to choose your courses. But stay relaxed. There's no need to decide your major, much less your life, as you get ready to register for your first term freshman year. Go into freshman year with an open mind; it's a time to experiment, to try things you never had a chance to in high school, to find out what you're good at, and to find out what you detest.

> We have a critical review that reviews most of the courses offered here that almost everyone uses. I've heard of freshmen who pack in really hard courses from the beginning of the semester. They probably don't understand that college classes are really different from high school ones. Some of them end up having to drop courses at the end of the semester.
>
> We also have an advising system that helps you with course selection. The school clips you with an upperclassman in your possible major, and that person gives you input on what courses are good or bad, and what courses are hard.
>
> — Junior, Brown University

Here are a few more guiding principles to keep in mind as you plan your semester.

The course catalog is your friend.

You'll receive your course catalog over the summer, probably some time in August. The typical course catalog provides information on core requirements and major requirements, and lists courses, course descriptions, professors, and meeting times. The course catalog is probably arranged alphabetically by department name, starting with something like "African American Studies" and ending with something like "Theatre Studies." Within the department listings, courses are probably numbered according to difficulty, beginning with introductory-level courses and prerequisites and ending with more advanced seminars or individual readings. You should pore through the course catalog over the summer when you have time and mark off possibilities. You can find out more about individual classes and professors once you get to school.

Tap into your academic advisor.
Academic advising varies wildly from college to college. Most colleges assign you a freshman academic advisor, probably faculty member, randomly, or based on the prospective major you put on your application. By your sophomore year, as your interests develop and you get to know faculty members, you'll probably get to choose your advisor. But for now, it's hit or miss. Hopefully, you attend a school with a functional advising system, and you end up with a helpful and accessible advisor. Unfortunately, even if you manage to hunt down your advisor and finagle a ten-minute appointment, at most schools they can't offer much information on topics outside of their departments. But you never know — your advisor could turn into your most valuable academic resource this side of Cliffs Notes, giving you info on core requirements, A.P. credits, and departments. So take the initial steps — be aggressive, make appointments, and ask questions. If your advisor isn't helpful, your academic dean, other freshmen, and older students might be.

Get core requirements out of the way early.
Some schools require that you demonstrate competency in a foreign language, take a term of physical education, or participate in a writing workshop in order to graduate. Others have a "core curriculum" or "distributional requirements," designed to ensure that you don't make it to graduation without sampling a variety of subjects outside your major. These core requirements typically mandate that you take one or more courses in each of several subjects or areas, such as philosophy, the fine arts, the social sciences, mathematics, and the laboratory sciences. At some schools, the core requirements are pretty hefty; the University of Chicago's Core, for instance, makes up more than half of all the credits required for graduation. Other schools require just a handful of courses in very broad subject areas. Whatever your situation, get the damn things out of the way early. You don't want to be stuck taking three science classes in your final semester or dealing with a foreign language requirement when you'd rather be deciding on or taking classes for your major. So take that required intro English class, that history survey, or basic calculus. Take the requirements

for what they're meant to be: an opportunity to experiment, to add breadth to your education, and to take courses that just look like they might float your boat.

Take placement exams and find out if Advanced Placement credit can get you out of a particular requirement.
Maybe the five years of swimming lessons your mom railroaded you into can spare you a term of ballroom dancing to meet your gym requirement. Maybe acing a placement exam or scoring a 4 or 5 on an A.P. exam can get you out of that pesky language requirement. Get all the info up front, before you register for a course that might substantially rehash work you did in high school.

Balance your schedule.
As a general rule, you don't want to overload your schedule with either too many humanities classes or too many math and science classes. Literature, history, and humanities-type classes tend to lay the reading and papers on thick, while science, math, or econ professors may bombard you with time-consuming and intensive weekly problem sets. Five problem sets due in one week versus five papers—it's hard to decide which is worse. Save yourself the anguish of finding out by keeping your schedule fairly balanced, both in terms of subject areas and in terms of course requirements.

Don't be afraid to branch out and experiment.
College, especially your first year, is a time to experiment. If your school has a pass/fail option, take advantage of it to explore courses you've had no exposure to. But whatever you do, if something in the course catalog catches your eye, don't avoid it simply because you know little about the subject. That random course in cultural anthropology could turn into one of the best classes you ever take. It could even turn into your major.

Find out about particular courses or professors before registration.
Don't pick a course based solely on the descriptions you read in the course catalog; those blurbs can make oral surgery sound like a little slice of heaven. What really matters is the professor—professors tend to develop reputations for being outstanding lecturers, for being disorganized, for having speech impediments. Get the dirt from older

students, your resident assistant, anyone who's willing to talk to you. Your R.A., in particular, can be one of your most valuable resources in your quest to obtain the dish on the courses and instructors that make your short list. Some schools also publish student-written course critiques that provide information on certain courses, including reading lists and grade distributions. Seek these out and let them be your guide.

COURSES FROM HELL

After you finish your first semester, you may be called upon to write evaluations of your courses for college course critique guides. Were the lectures helpful? Did you like the textbook? Would you recommend the course to a friend? Here is a selection of particularly negative responses to courses that the students evidently didn't like, taken from one school's course critique.

- "Text makes a satisfying 'thud' when dropped on the floor."
- "Textbook is confusing. Someone with a knowledge of English should proofread it."
- "Have you ever fallen asleep in class and awoke in another? That's the way I felt all term."
- "It was so confusing that I forgot who I was, where I was, and what I was doing—It's a great stress reliever."
- "I would sit in class and stare out the window at the squirrels. They've got a cool nest in the tree."
- "TA steadily improved throughout the course. I think he started drinking and it really loosened him up."

Take advantage of electronic resources.
Many instructors post reading lists, course syllabi, or course requirements on the college or university Web site. These Internet listings can be extremely helpful in mapping out your semester; it's always better to find out you'll have 400 pages of weekly reading for a course before you elect it, rather than after.

Consider taking an introductory writing workshop or class in basic prose. Many colleges now require a writing or introductory prose class for freshmen. Even if your school doesn't, consider taking one. It's an opportunity to take a small, workshop-style class, as well as develop skills and set a foundation you'll need no matter what you choose to concentrate on in college. Not all high schools prepare students to write the way they're expected to in college, and your first couple of papers will probably not be pretty. A prose class can teach you what to expect and how to deliver.

"Guts"; "easy-As"; "blowoffs"; "GPA-boosters"—by whatever name you call them, they smell as sweet. Courses like "Rocks for Jocks" (geology for non-majors), "Clapping for Credit" (introductory music), "Physics for Poets," "Kiddy Chem," and "Math for Plants" have brightened many a college student's semester, and, of course, grade point average. Every campus has its bevy of courses and professors that achieves some level of notoriety, or popularity, depending on how you look at it, because of easier-than-average requirements and/or grading. But proceed with caution—the class you are about to take may not be as easy as you've heard, or as easy as its title might suggest. Slack excessively, and the results may not be pretty. But once in a while, if you're taking a demanding schedule; if the class or professor seem really interesting; hell, if you just need a break—go ahead, indulge. Following are a few of the more interesting-sounding guts (and the nicknames by which they are more popularly known) at schools across the country:

- The Concept of Hero in Greek Civilization (Heroes for Zeroes), Harvard University
- Visual Thinking 1 (Cut and Paste), University of Chicago
- Physics 100 (Funhundred), Williams College
- Alcohol and Other Drugs in American Culture (Beer Gut), Yale University

SCHEDULING

As you look ahead in terms of distributional requirements and potential major requirements, consider what your daily schedule will be like. Here are some tips to help you keep your schedule sane:

Don't take too many classes.
Most schools require four to five classes per semester; there's no need to tackle more than that. First-semester freshman year is traditionally an "adjustment" year when it comes to academics; the transition from high school work to college work may take you by surprise, and you don't want to bite off more than you can chew by taking six classes. At the same time, don't take too few classes; try to leave enough room that you can

comfortably drop a class that you're, say, miserably failing, without landing yourself on academic probation. Your school's add/drop policies are probably printed somewhere in the course catalog, but if they're not, you can ask your advisor, college dean, or R.A. for help.

Think realistically about the earliest class you want to take.
Yes, you got up at 6 A.M. for swim practice every morning in high school and made it to class bright-eyed and chipper by 7:45. But college is like a different temporal dimension, an alternate universe in which getting up for a 9 A.M. class becomes a mighty struggle, and, more often than not, a losing battle. College students tend go to bed (much) later than high school students. Unless the course is a real winner, and you are extremely disciplined, find a later class. The snooze button is an alluring alternative to an early, possibly boring lecture three times a week.

Make sure you schedule lunch.
Every day. Cramming in back-to-back classes in the middle of the day is one of the biggest mistakes freshmen make. It's bad enough if you skip breakfast, but if you skip lunch too, you will be positively drained and unfocused by early afternoon.

Pay attention to where your classes are.
Typically, there's a space of ten to 15 minutes between standard class meeting slots. If all the classroom buildings are located in the same general vicinity, this is not a problem. But if you're going to be booking from one end of campus to another, you may want to think again. Professors tend to get annoyed when you arrive late to their classes, even if you are red-faced and panting when you stumble through the door.

MAJORS AND MINORS

You've heard it repeated over and over again, like some sort of weird mantra: You don't have to choose your major right away . . . take your time . . . explore your options. But picking a major will probably lurk stealthily just beneath the surface of your consciousness at all times, like a splinter in your toe. So here's the deal: everything you always wanted to know about majors, double majors, triple majors, interdisciplinary majors, self-designed majors. And let's not forget minors. Double minors, triple minors, interdisciplinary minors . . . OK, you get the point.

Virtually all colleges and universities require you to concentrate or specialize in a subject of your choice. A major is usually associated with a particular department at a college or university, and you typically have to take a certain number of courses in that department in order to graduate. In some cases, you'll have to take prerequisites, basic foundational courses in a subject, before you can declare your major. And usually, there are specific courses or types of courses required for each major, as well as some sort of painful senior requirement or thesis. For example, an English major at Yale has to take 14 courses (36 courses total are required for graduation) in the English department. Either one year-long introductory class in English poetry or four separate poetry courses are required, along with four courses that deal with literature before 1800. Finally, English majors have to meet a senior requirement, either by writing a 25-page paper in a special senior seminar, or writing a 30–40 page senior essay outside of a class.

While most majors are affiliated with a department, some schools offer interdisciplinary majors, where students take classes in a variety of departments. For example, an African American studies major might be required to take certain courses in the history, literature, or sociology departments. Some universities, like Brown, give students the option of designing their own major, if the school doesn't offer one that meets their interests. For instance, a student might design a major in something like "Cultural Studies" or "Philosophy and Math." Don't get any strange ideas, though—a proposed major in "Human Sexual Behavior" probably won't wash. Usually, students who design such alternative concentrations have to get them approved and reviewed by an academic committee, which often imposes even more rigorous requirements than those for ordinary majors.

Another alternative is completing a double major, by fulfilling the requirements for two separate major programs. The two majors can be complementary in some way, such as political science and international relations, or they can be completely distinct from each other, like computer science and history. In either case, though, it's pretty hard to double major at most schools and still meet all your core or distributional requirements. Unless you're willing to take pretty heavy course loads every semester or attend summer school, cramming it in in just four years can be a real sacrifice. What double majors gain in depth they lose in breadth; although they have two areas of intense concentration, they don't get to take a wide variety of classes outside their majors. If your school allows you to choose a minor, or even two minors, as does NYU, consider this alternative. A minor is a subconcentration or specialization that requires fewer courses than a major, but still allows you to study a subject in some depth.

One last word about majors: You will change yours. Probably more than once. Maybe you'll get a D in one of the prerequisites. Maybe you'll find out you don't like cutting up hamsters. Maybe you'll discover a latent fascination with Near Eastern religions. Don't worry—this is common, and even good. As long as you make up your mind early enough to take all the courses you need for your major, it's fine to change your mind.

SPECIAL CONSIDERATIONS FOR SCIENCE MAJORS

If you think you're going to major in science, you have do a little more planning ahead than prospective humanities majors your freshman year. While humanities majors typically don't declare their majors until junior year or later, most science majors declare sophomore year. Natural science departments generally have more prerequisites than other departments, and many of these prerequisites are year-long courses. So if you don't get your act together and your schedule exactly right the first time around, you can't be a bio major, you will never get into medical school, and your life will be ruined.

Just kidding, just kidding. But seriously, if you are planning or even thinking of majoring in science, review the department's requirements, talk to your academic advisor or dean extensively, and attend any and all advising sessions your school offers for possible science majors. Schools normally hold these advising sessions during orientation week and/or the first week of classes, so take some time out from building your loft or waiting on line to check one out. You'll find out exactly what you need to do, and most likely have the opportunity to ask science faculty and administrators questions. These meetings can be invaluable. It's generally true that in order to fulfill all the requirements of a natural science major, you'll have to take at least one science class freshman year. If you've been inspired by *E.R.* and think you might want to be premed, your first-year schedule may be slightly more constrained than the typical freshman's.

The Wacky World of Premed

Some colleges have interdisciplinary premedical programs, or, like Boston University and Washington University in St. Louis, offer seven- or eight-year combined undergraduate–medical school programs for exceptional students. In most cases, though, students fulfill the requirements for any major they choose and then take the additional courses that medical schools require for admission. The classes required by most medical schools are pretty standard; you need, at minimum, one full year each of intro chem, introductory bio, intro physics, and organic chemistry, all with laboratory. You'll probably also have to take one semester of calculus and at least one English class. Contrary to what you might have heard, writing ability is really important to medical schools. In addition, some schools recommend, but don't require, a course in biochemistry. A.P. credits do not fulfill these requirements, but usually, they allow you to place into a more advanced level of a course. For example, if your school offers two levels of introductory chemistry, and you scored a 5 on the A.P. chem exam, the higher level might be more appropriate for you.

Generally, as a freshman, you'll want to take either or both intro chem and intro bio, with lab(s). Also, it's good to take the calculus class right away, since math skills tend to go bye-bye if not used. But again, to figure out what you need to take freshman year, hound your advisor with questions and drag your butt to those premed counseling sessions.

If you decide to major in a natural science, such as biology, chemistry, or physics, you'll probably meet those specific requirements just by completing your major. But remember, you don't have to major in science to be pre-med. Only about half of all medical school applicants majored in science as undergrads. As a matter of fact, schools generally want to see candidates who, while demonstrating strong science skills and preparation, are also academically well rounded and have varied interests. So don't declare yourself a bio major on the first day of classes freshman year just because you think it will up your chances of getting into med school; relax, explore, and take your time figuring out what you want to concentrate in.

THE BASICS OF COURSE SURVIVAL

The alarm clock rings, interrupting your peaceful slumber with blaring insistence. The snooze button beckons seductively, and the sole thought that penetrates your dazed consciousness is "ten more minutes."

An hour and a half later, you stumble out of bed and into the shower, sobered by the thought of the long day that lies ahead of you.

You've got class.

Once classes start, dragging yourself out of bed is the least of the challenges you'll face. From dissecting your syllabus, to wading through rivers of reading, to dealing with your distant professor, the pressure of collegiate academia can overwhelm you at first. This chapter takes you through the basics of course survival, from choosing a section to devising a schedule.

> I find there is certainly more work in college in high school, but you also have so much more time to do it. You are actually in class about half as much in college and you sleep less. But nothing in high school compares to the final exam period, especially the last three weeks of first semester.
>
> —Sophomore, Yale University

THE SETTING

There are two basic blueprints for college courses: lectures, and seminars or workshops. Lecture-style courses, in which a professor delivers several lectures a week to anywhere from 25 to 400 students, dominate at many larger universities; introductory and required classes, in particular, are typically large, crowded lectures. For freshmen who are used to the more personal, one-on-one attention from high school instructors, one-, two-, or three-hundred-person lectures often seem cold and impersonal; it may be harder for you to learn if you feel that you're just one face in a vast ocean.

Your school will try to alleviate this problem by dividing students in large lecture courses into smaller, probably mandatory, discussion groups called sections or recitations. A section is led by a teaching assistant (T.A.), a graduate student who has at least some background in the course material, or a tangentially related field. In most lecture classes, a T.A. will grade your papers and exams, meaning you'll have little to no personal contact with the professor. While an outstanding (or particularly attractive) teaching assistant can salvage a mediocre course, what you take out of a lecture class depends largely on the professor. A bored-sounding, aloof lecturer who is either embarrassingly unprepared or reads in a maddening monotone from a stack of notecards can suck the marrow out of the most interesting subject. On the other hand, an engaging professor with a dynamic lecturing style can make you forget you're sitting in a lecture hall larger than your local movie theater. That's why it's so important to find out as much as you can about the instructor before you elect a course.

Seminars or workshops are smaller, usually professor-led classes of about 10 to 20 students. At some large universities, coveted spots in seminars or colloquia go to upperclassmen first, but you should make every effort to get into as many of these smaller-sized courses as possible. Some smaller universities and liberal arts colleges offer these courses almost exclusively, and others offer professor-taught seminars specifically for freshmen. Seminars are an opportunity to take a small class with an experienced professor, get feedback from someone who's probably an expert in his or her field, and learn the course material in a more intimate and personal setting.

THE PLAYERS

Professors

Leave memories of your old high school teachers buried in the pages of your yearbook. College professors are a whole other breed.

> I had this professor for a Soviet communism class who was definitely a communist himself. He said we could do three extra credit papers over the course of the semester and he would add 10 points to our final grade. Not only did he not count the three papers at all, but no matter how hard I studied, I got the same grade for everything. I guess everyone had to get the same grade; you know, the communist way.
>
> —Junior, Columbia University

Professors are like a box of chocolates. You never know what you're gonna get. Some deliver their lectures dutifully, ending them after precisely one hour to head for the lab or work on the book. Others encourage dialogue, welcome students at frequent office hours, or invite classes to their homes for potluck dinners. Different styles, different attitudes, different philosophies . . . you'll click with some and not with others, but there are a few general things you can expect.

College professors are obviously experts in their field; they wouldn't be on the faculty if they weren't. Most of them are sincerely enthusiastic about passing that interest on to their their students, and most of them are more accessible than they appear. But professors usually have projects besides teaching on their plates, activities that place heavy demands on their time and energy, time and energy they can't devote to teaching undergraduate classes.

Maybe your history professor is working on his fifth book and dealing with pressure from his department to publish. Maybe your chemistry professor is spending long hours in the lab doing research. The point is, it may take a little time, effort, and patience to establish a good relationship with your professor. In most cases, it's definitely worth it.

There's a world of difference between developing a good relationship with your professor and bowing so low you scrape your head on the ground. Blatant ass kissing is irritating to both the professor and everyone else in your class. That's not to say you shouldn't get on the big guy's good side; he is, after all, giving you your grade. You just don't want to be offensive or degrade yourself in the process. If you're in a small seminar with a professor, stay on his or her good side by coming to class (preferably on time). Don't be cocky or confrontational in class, but don't feel obliged to nod dumbly at everything that comes out of your professor's mouth like it's the gospel truth, either. If you strongly disagree with something a professor says, don't be afraid to challenge her, even she did win a Nobel Prize in her field. Even when she chews you up and spits you out like stick of Juicy Fruit, she'll probably respect you for trying. Caution: Don't even try this if you don't know exactly what you're talking about; in most college class discussions, empty rhetoric just doesn't fly. If you have a legitimate question, concern, or comment, don't hesitate to go to the professor's weekly office hours and bring it up there; he or she will be happy to see you're thinking critically about the course material and investing time in the class. On the other hand, showing up weekly to expound on your fascination with the course work is neither necessary nor constructive. Generally, professors want to know that you're interested in the subject matter and are making some effort to absorb it. One of the best ways you can do this is by coming to class, and coming prepared.

Class participation, which is usually factored somehow into your grade, is key in these seminars. You could get away with keeping your mouth shut a lot more easily in high school than you can in college; your professor will simply not buy that you're deep in silent contemplation. More likely, he'll assume that you haven't done the reading. This is bad. If you really don't have time to do the reading, at least try to skim it. This way, you can formulate a thoughtful and articulate comment or two and dazzle the class with brilliance before your professor has a chance to ask you a question. Be careful, though—B.S. can carry you only so far, and some professors are pretty good with a shovel. If you actually have prepared for the class, but you're naturally shy or quiet, it can be agonizing to speak up, especially if the professor has an intimidating teaching style, or tends to engage students in debate. Again, try to prepare an intelligent question or comment before you get to class. As you do the reading, take notes in the margins to cue you once the discussion starts. If you have a reaction to something another student says, take a deep breath and *spit it out*. It's not easy, but the only way you'll become more comfortable with this crucial aspect of college life is by forcing yourself to do it. Again, if you tend toward the other direction and enjoy the sound of your own voice a little too much, try to rein in your tongue. You know something's wrong if you find yourself talking more than the professor. He does, after all, have a Ph.D. in the subject, and probably a whole lot more to say.

As a final note, keep in mind that professors are people, too. Although relationships with professors are generally more formal that those with high school teachers, they're also more adult. You shouldn't be intimidated or afraid to hang out once in a while. Take your cues from the professor; many eat in the dining hall or attend student functions, and you can sometimes take this as an opportunity to get to know your professors on a social level, and to show them you have a dimension beyond what they see in class. And when a course is over, stay in touch with professors you forged a good relationship with; in the future, they can provide valuable advice, connections, and recommendations.

Teaching Assistants
T.A.'s are primarily graduate students pursuing their Ph.D.'s. The good news is, most of them want to be professors (what else would you do with a Ph.D. in Russian literature?). The bad news is, they're not.

If a university's first-rate faculty was one of its biggest lures for you, you might be disappointed when graduate students are doing a lot of the "teaching." If you're lucky, the T.A. will be leading sections for a course that deals with their specialty, has T.A.'d for that course in the past, and has elected to teach undergraduates. In the worst-case scenario, a T.A. is teaching a course to meet some sort of requirement, and has little background in the field. In these circumstances, T.A.'s learn the material as they go along, furiously scribbling lecture notes alongside undergrads, and reading the course books for the first time. To make matters worse, experiences with T.A.'s vary even more widely than they do with professors—most graduate students don't teach long enough to develop reputations.

In theory, T.A.'s and discussion sections are intended to supplement the course, not make up the substance of it. Most of the time, though, you'll find that your main contact for a large lecture course is the teaching fellow.

The same guidelines that apply for dealing with professors also go for teaching assistants. With T.A.'s (who tend to have fairly big, but sensitive, egos), it may be even more important that you attend the section regularly; attendance and participation almost always count toward your grade, and graduate students tend to take it pretty personally if no one shows up for their sections. They're kind of touchy that way.

THE GAME PLAN

You've got the setting and the players down; now it's time for the game plan, the how-to. Here are some general tips to guide you on the rocky road to academic nirvana; more specific information on exams, study habits, and papers will follow in the next two chapters.

Schedule, schedule, schedule.
Get an academic planner. Or treat yourself to one of those stupid desk calendars. Or program your computer to let you know the night before you have a major assignment due. Do anything you have to to keep the dates straight. When you're filling in your calendar for the semester, pore over your syllabus—a chronological and detailed listing of lectures, readings, assignments, exams, and other requirements for a course. It's never pretty when you miss an assignment. It's even less pretty when you remember at 11 the night before. So do yourself a favor and write those dates down somewhere where you'll check them. You might as well put your mom's birthday on there too, while you're at it.

Go to class.
Yeah, it's pretty obvious, but when that snooze button caressingly whispers your name, the temptation to bag can be overpowering. Going to class, whether lecture, seminar, or section, is the most painless way to bolster the old G.P.A. And while you're there, take a note or two.

Take notes.
You're halfway through your midterm exam. You've gone to class, done most of the reading, and in short, you're cruisin'. Suddenly you come

across a question that might as well be written in Latin (and this is not a Latin class). It's so out of left field, you later ask a classmate what the hell the professor was thinking. The inevitable answer: "He said it in lecture."

For some people, note taking in high school was sort of optional. You could remember important stuff off the top of your head, and test questions were normally pulled right from the textbooks anyway. Not so in college. In most classes, taking complete, legible, lecture notes is as important as doing the reading. Professors lecture on topics not covered in the reading, and ask very specific questions drawn from lectures on the exams—partly for reasons of ego, and partly to make sure you went to class. So as you sit in class and your mind begins to wander to this weekend and your eyes begin to wander to the person sitting two rows ahead of you, force yourself to tune in. Remember that while your doodles won't help you on the final, lecture notes probably will. Don't try to transcribe each lecture; you'll be suffering hand spasms by the time the hour's up. Copy down anything at all that makes it to a blackboard. Write down main ideas and repeated catchphrases, especially ones that you don't understand, like "rational choice theory." Develop your own abbreviations and shorthand. And finally, beg your friends or classmates for their notes if you miss lecture so you can have a complete set.

Do the reading (or at least skim it).

As you flip through page after page of the document your professor calls a reading list, reality sets in with brutal force: You will never finish your reading. It simply isn't possible. Sure, for the first week or so, you may neatly underline pertinent passages in all your textbooks. You may stay up late preparing outlines or summaries of the assigned chapter/volumes/novels. You may (gasp!) do the suggested readings. Alas, this cannot continue long—when the assignments start piling up, you won't have the time or energy to pore through the reading with the thoroughness of an ancient scribe. The important thing, though, is not to let yourself fall too far behind. And it's a slippery slope, my friend. You fall so far behind and let the reading pile up so high that you feel you'll never catch up . . . so you fall further behind and let the reading pile up even higher. What you want to do is just plow your way through the reading; if time is really limited, read the first few pages, the last few pages, and lightly skim everything in between. It's not ideal, and you should try to catch up at some later point (read: finals week), but it's better than not even knowing what poet you're on or what war you're up to.

ALPHABET SOUP

Grades. Can a transcript full of letters really reflect what you've learned in college? Don't personal growth and satisfaction count for anything? Besides, D is for Diploma, right? Do grades really matter, anyway?

Please. You wouldn't be facing reality—or reading this book, for that matter—if you didn't think the answer was a big, fat, resounding, earth-shattering, reverberating *yes*. Your transcript will follow you throughout your academic life and the early part of your professional career. Grades matter to graduate and professional schools. They matter to future employers. They matter to agencies and foundations that award scholarships to students with high G.P.A.'s. They matter to your parents, who are not paying an arm and a leg to watch you rack up the Fs. And most of all, they matter to you.

Getting good grades in your courses is most likely your highest priority in college, and rightly so. Usually, grades are a good measure of how hard you've worked and how much you've learned (though not always!). And there's no better measure than the cumulative G.P.A.

The Grade Point Average (G.P.A.)

The vast majority of colleges and universities calculate a grade point average based on a four-point scale. Most schools convert letter grades to a grade point by awarding one third of a point for each third of a letter grade, in the following way:

A = 4.00	C+ = 2.33
A– = 3.67	C = 2.00
B+ = 3.33	D+ = 1.67
B = 3.00	D = 1.00
B– = 2.67	D– = 0.67

Grades of A+ usually convert to either a 4 or a 4.33, and schools don't award any credit for an F. To figure out your G.P.A., convert each letter grade you've received into a number using the four-point scale, and multiply each by the number of credits the course was worth. Next, add up the point total and divide by the total number of credits, and, *voila*, you've got your G.P.A. Some schools use a different system to calculate the cumulative G.P.A., but the one described is pretty much standard.

The Pass/Fail Option

Some schools allow you take a certain number of courses toward your graduation requirement on a pass/fail basis. Such grades are not calculated into your cumulative G.P.A., but they'll appear on your transcript with a P or (shudder) an F next to the course name. If you're really lucky, you go to a school where freshmen take *all* their classes pass/fail first semester. If not, find out how many courses you can take pass/fail, and milk the option for all it's worth. You don't want to have *too* many pass/fail grades on your transcript, but the option can give you the opportunity to explore unfamiliar subjects or take courses you might not want to take for a grade.

STRESS AND TIME MANAGEMENT

Balancing a heavier academic workload than you've ever had and dealing with all kinds of new feelings can take its emotional toll. As you juggle papers, exams, new friends, old friends, and everything else in your life, you sense that feeling coming on. That feeling that the end is not in sight. That feeling that your head is going to implode. That feeling called *stress*.

Stress is a normal and inevitable part of college life. Some amount of stress is actually necessary—we all need it to motivate us as that paper deadline or big midterm approaches. Too much stress, though, can be counterproductive; it can keep you from tackling your classes, retaining material, and recalling information on test day. Even more important, it can take its toll on your physical and mental health. There are a few things you can do to minimize your academic stress; one of them is to manage your time effectively.

Scheduling

Once again, it's really important to mark important dates in a calendar or planner and check them frequently. If at the beginning of the semester you learn you have two papers and a problem set due the last week in November, at least you'll have some time to plan. You can make an effort to begin researching one or both of the papers in advance, and avoid feeling panicked or overwhelmed during that week.

Procrastination

College students across continents have turned procrastination into a science. No matter how much time you have for an assignment and no matter how big or how small the task is, the temptation to leave it to the last possible moment can be very strong. When it comes to papers, we complacently assume that we can churn them out in whatever time we have left, be it two weeks, two days, or two hours. Sure, producing the sheer volume is no problem, but it's impossible to produce sophisticated, polished work in one night. Even if you're doing well, chances are you're not doing as well as you could be. And when it comes to exams, procrastination can really leave its ugly, indelible imprint all over your transcript; to put off studying for a cumulative midterm or final exam is begging to crash and burn.

You will never slay the heinous beast that is procrastination; it's completely normal and perfectly understandable. But don't let it escalate to the point that you can't handle your workload. Set realistic, short-term goals for yourself. In college, reading assignments tend to be more open-ended than they were in high school—you may not know exactly when those four books of *The Aeneid* are due, just that you're responsible for reading them. It becomes very easy to fall behind and never catch up. So resolve to finish those books by a certain date. If you have a paper due, set a date to have the research done, or a complete outline, or a draft. Reward yourself for meeting a series of those goals with a night off.

ACADEMIC TROUBLE

If you do find yourself falling behind in your classes and think you might even be in danger of not passing, deal with the situation as soon as you know you're in trouble. Talk first to your R.A., dean, or advisor, especially if depression, emotional problems, or physical illness has been keeping you from doing well. If you're simply not grasping the course material but have made a legitimate effort, discuss the problem with your professor. Chances are he will be sympathetic. With the exception of a wicked few, professors generally don't enjoy giving failing grades, especially if a student has worked hard or has a legitimate reason for not completing work satisfactorily. Soap opera addiction does not qualify.

If you're not able to complete the requirements of a class because of some extreme situation, such as a family emergency or extreme illness, your professor or dean can give you a temporary incomplete in a class, which appears on your transcript as an "I" until you finish the work. When there's absolutely no hope, when you know will never be able to pull yourself out of the abyss for a particular class, you may want to consider withdrawing. Most schools allow you to withdraw from a course until very late in the semester. You'll probably get a "W" on your transcript, which doesn't look great, so don't make a habit out of it. But needless to say, it looks far better than an "F."

Remember that if you have a genuine reason for failing to hand in work or for doing poorly, your R.A., counselors, and professors will, in most cases, be supportive. Vocalize your concerns and try to address them early, before things get completely out of hand. Everybody falls behind at some point, especially during freshman year, when there's just so much to deal with. But if it reaches a point at which you're not even meeting the minimum requirements for a course, you need to talk to someone right away before the damage becomes irreparable.

EXAMS

Exam. It's every college student's favorite four-letter word, and the very sound of it may be enough to make your palms sweat and your blood pressure rise.

In college, your grades aren't based on countless nightly homework assignments and weekly quizzes that, taken alone, each account for only a fraction of your grade. Instead, you have exams—big, fat, scary exams. Sure, in some courses, several requirements combine to determine your grade; maybe you'll have a paper, a presentation or two, a class participation grade, a series of problem sets. But in others, particularly in the sciences, your grade is based almost exclusively on your performance on a midterm or a series of midterms, and on the final.

No pressure, though.

Basically, this just means that you need a crash course on how to study effectively, the various test formats and types of question, and how to rake in maximum points when the blue books start flying.

STUDY TACTICS
There's no getting around it. Sooner or later you're going to need to study. Ideally, you don't want to be cracking the spine of your textbook the night before your first midterm, or worse, before the final. Not enough sleep and too much caffeine will lower your concentration and make it tough for you

to recall facts or write an analytical essay when the clock starts. So you don't want to resort to an all-nighter; there's nothing worse than watching the sun rise as you realize you have inexplicably managed to fry your brain *and* absorb absolutely nothing. Of course, one of the easiest and most effective ways you can prepare for exams is by going to class, staying (however precariously) on top of the reading, and taking good notes. For science and math classes, there's probably no better preparation than struggling through weekly or biweekly problem sets. As the exam approaches though, you'll need to start reviewing more intensively.

Pick a Spot, Any Spot

One of the most important things you can do when it comes to studying is finding yourself a spot. Why, I'll have my room, you say.

Weeeell, not likely. If you're a freshman and your name is not Chelsea Clinton, you probably will not have a single. Which means if you try to study in your room you're going to have to deal with one huge, walking, talking, distraction. Your roommate may be sleeping, studying, playing music, or having sex at all sorts of inconvenient times. Even more of a problem is the fact that your bedroom contains, by definition, a bed. Your bed, with its innocently fluffy pillows and soft, downy comforter, is in reality your mortal enemy when you are attempting to study. Avoid it as you would a poisonous snake.

You *can* give studying in your room a try; who knows, you may find it works for you. But if you are forced to eliminate your room as a study possibility, you're not left with too many options. The most obvious one, of course, is the library. Virtually all college libraries have designated study spaces. You can probably choose from a variety of library study spots, from lounges with big, comfy chairs, to open spaces with tables, to tiny, private study cubicles ("weenie bins").

Experiment and find what's right for you. Maybe you need the privacy and quiet of a weenie bin. Maybe you study best while sitting in the TV lounge (I don't recommend it). Maybe you like the quiet buzz or "white noise" of a coffeehouse or a courtyard. The important thing is that you find a spot that allows you to focus for long periods of time, that doesn't harbor too many distractions, and that, of course, is fairly safe and public.

Get into the habit of studying in the same surroundings consistently; this might help you settle into your "study mode" and concentrate better.

Study Tips

You've staked out your turf in the library and are ready to get started. If you've attended every class, taken impeccable notes, and have underlined, highlighted, and summarized all the readings, congratulations. I hope you and your flash cards have a wonderful life together. If you have a little more work ahead of you, welcome to college!

> I can now get away with studying less, because I know what I need to do, what I don't need to do, and the stuff I need to read. Teaching Assistants can help you find out what material you must concentrate on to do well on exams. Studying for exams in groups works, because you can split the readings and workload you must do. Also, if you are one of those people who hasn't gone to lectures, but did the readings, you can trade notes and thoughts with someone who did the opposite.
>
> —Junior, Harvard University

Different people have all kinds of different study methods; the important thing is figuring out what techniques work for you, and how you need to tailor them to different courses and vary them for different test formats. Here are some basic things you might want to try, beyond reviewing your lecture notes and rescanning the reading:

- For starters, ask a friend for his or her notes on lectures you might have missed. Grovel if you must. And if the test is rapidly approaching, skim any reading you haven't yet done. Even if time is scarce, try to at least expose yourself to pretty much everything that's covered in the class. Maybe remembering a catchphrase or a small detail will help you B.S. your way through an essay, or take a mildly educated guess at a passage I.D.

- If your class requires a lot of memorization, such as vocabulary for a French class, paintings and dates for an art history class, or chemical formulas for an intro chem class, try making flash cards. Just writing down the information on index cards can help you absorb some of it. The important thing to note, though, is that you're not going to be able to memorize 200 paintings, artists, and dates in one night. It's a cumulative process. If you already had a midterm in the class, you've probably learned a lot of the material already and just need to refresh your memory; if the final is the first time you'll have to regurgitate a lot of facts and details, you'll need discipline. Start studying in advance.

- If they're available, look for past exams. Professors, especially in the sciences, sometimes give out old exams; sometimes they're available in the library; and sometimes your T.A. can provide you one or two. Looking at an old exam will give you a feel for what information you're supposed to know and how much detail you'll be expected to go into. You'll also get a feel for the format and for the professor's style. If you've gotten a copy of an old science or math exam, do the questions or problems in it. While the numbers or details may be different, the methodology behind solving the problems will probably be similar.

- To prepare for science, math, or econ sets, look over your problem sets, and rework the questions on them. Your professor will probably ask similar questions on the exam.

- Go to optional review sessions, especially those lead by T.A.'s. T.A.'s will give you at least some general information about what will be on the test just as a reward for showing up. And more often than not, they'll let some juicy tidbit inadvertently slip, possibly saving you some valuable study time. Review sessions also give you the opportunity to set up or join study groups with other students in the class.

- Give a study group a try. Warning: Study groups do not work for everyone. You may not be comfortable preparing for a test with other students. And inevitably, some people in a group are going to be, ahem, less prepared than others. But it can't really hurt to meet briefly with other students to share notes and information, and discuss broad themes that might provide fodder for an essay on exam day.

- If all else fails, look for short cuts. Read the introductions and conclusions of all your assigned chapters. If you know that someone else takes better notes than you, ask to borrow them. Of course, the lender is not always thrilled about this; someone we knew junior year walked into class the day of the midterm to find twelve xeroxed copies of her incredibly detailed lecture notes floating through the room. She was not pleased.

- Remain calm. Please extinguish all cigarettes. An oxygen mask will drop from an overhead compartment, and you may use seat cushion as a flotation device . . . Oh. Sorry. Wrong crisis. Seriously, though, don't panic, especially if you've pretty much kept up throughout the semester.

Again, it's really crucial that you find a study system that works for you. You might like to work chronologically through the syllabus, you might like to work thematically, you might like flash cards, or outlines, or summaries. It'll probably take you a while to develop effective study habits. Give yourself adequate time to do it. And whatever you do, don't leave it all for the night before.

> Because at college you procratistinate a lot more, cramming becomes both necessary and inevitable. When the time comes for you to cram, find a place that is isolated so that you don't get distracted, and concentrate on one topic at a time, because you are in really deep trouble right now. Although you might be pulling all-nighters the day before the exam, make sure you get frequent breaks to rest your mind, and do not stress out, because stressing out can lower your capacity to cram.
>
> —Freshman, Smith College

THE ALL-NIGHTER: SO MANY PAGES, SO LITTLE TIME

It's a ritual as old as college itself, as familiar to students as bad food and shrunken laundry.

It's the all-nighter.

College students around the globe have elevated the all-nighter to an art form and speak of it in hushed and reverent tones. Pulling a successful all-nighter commands a certain level of respect and elicits a certain level of sympathy from fellow students.

It also stinks in a big way.

Let's be clear. Nobody should do this, even though everybody does. If you pull an all-nighter before an exam, the fatigue and the large amounts of caffeine you may have consumed will act against you on the test. Your eyes will be tired, your hands will ache, you'll have trouble getting your newly memorized facts straight, and you won't be able to synthesize a coherent essay. Pulling an all-nighter to finish a paper is not great, but it's not nearly as bad as pulling one the night before an exam.

> I've had to pull nine all-nighters in two weeks, and it was definitely not fun. But I see it this way: If you don't have good notes, haven't gone to classes, and don't even have the books, you have three options: 1) cheat 2) drop out of school or 3) cram. Of the options, the first is of course illegal, and can lead to a forced result of option two. And many people (including your parents) won't be too happy if you take the second options just because you couldn't get off your butt and study during the entire semester. So, you are left with option three.
>
> —Junior, Yale University

Here are some tips for maximizing coverage and minimizing physical pain the night before an exam for which you are woefully ill-prepared:

- First of all, don't plan to be up *all* night. Three or four little hours spent sleeping will be infinitely more valuable to you than the pitiful amount of reading you'd be able to struggle through in that time. Tell yourself you will study for so many hours, and sleep for four.

I remember the time when I kept putting off my studying and had to pull off several all-nighters during finals. I felt good about my studying and tackled those exams. But, being sleepless did have its price. I found myself dozing in the middle of one of them. Preparing for any exam means being physically ready as well—try to get at least a little sleep.

—Junior, University of California, Los Angeles

- During your designated study time, *stay away from your bed*. It is evil. And for God's sake, don't study in it. 'Tis certain doom. As a matter of fact, just avoid your room completely. Study in your common room, the library, a study lounge, the TV room (don't worry, no one will be over there at 4 A.M.). Anywhere, really, as long as your mattress is at a safe distance.

- If you find yourself drifting off, try that multipurpose remedy, the cold shower.

- Go easy on the caffeine. When you know you'll be watching the sun come up in a few hours, it's tempting to drown yourself in rivers of caffeinated beverages like coffee, Jolt™ or Mountain Dew™, or eat a bag of chocolate-covered coffee beans. If you feel the urge, go ahead and take a coffee break, or eat a candy bar—it'll give you a chance to rest your eyes and maybe give you a second wind. But consume in moderation, because too much caffeine can be counterproductive. It can destroy your concentration and make you as jittery as the Energizer™ Bunny.

- Set your alarm clock *really loud*. As loud as it goes. Trust me, when you're going on three to four hours of sleep, you want that thing blaring in your ear. And don't put it right next to the bed; you don't want to turn it off in your sleep-deprived and drowsy state and wake up five minutes before (or five minutes after) your exam starts.

CAFFEINE: THE COLLEGE STUDENT'S DRUG OF CHOICE

Here are the caffeine levels of various substances, in milligrams. As your all-nighter progresses, you may tempted to hook yourself up to a Mountain Dew IV. Consume caffeine sparingly, though—too much of it can act against you at test time.

Vivarin	200 mg
Coffee (brewed, 7 oz.)	80–135
Coffee (instant, 7oz)	65–100
Jolt (12-oz. can)	71.2
Coca-Cola (12-oz. can)	45.6
Chocolate bar	30
Cold relief tablet	30
7-Up	0

—Source: Alex Lopez-Ortiz, University of Waterloo

IT'S BLUE-BOOK TIME

Examination. course examination; oral examination; multiple-choice examination; comprehensive examination; midterm examination; final examination; take-home examination; unannounced examination.

—Entries under "examination" from Roget's International Thesaurus

Some exams consist of just one type of test question, such as essay or short answer, but more often than not they'll pack a combination punch. Maybe you'll get a short-answer section, followed by one or two longer essays. Following are descriptions of various of types of exams designed to bring you to your knees—that is, evaluate your grasp of the material.

Short-answer exams

The good news is that these tests, designed to measure your grasp of the facts and detail of the course, leave little room for subjectivity; if you work hard and know your stuff, it'll be reflected in your grade. The bad news is, there's also little room for B.S. You can't dance around the question; if you don't know what *Limbo* is in Dante's *Inferno,* you won't get partial credit for a lengthy discussion on party games. It's that simple. Short-answer questions come in a few basic forms—multiple-choice or multiple-guess (when in doubt, pick C); true-false (be grateful if you see these in college); passage identifications (identify the work from which a cited passage is drawn); and plain old questions that you're expected to answer in just a word or a sentence or two.

Essays
Essay questions are extremely common, and often one or two long essays make up an entire exam. Here's an essay question from the midterm exam in an international relations class on ethics:

"The essential dilemma behind all ethical theories of war and conflict is the tension between doing harm and allowing harm to be done."

Defend or refute this statement, drawing on specific examples from the thinkers we've read so far.

Reread the question and look for clues about what you're expected to do. You're given a statement, forced to make a judgment on it, and asked to incorporate specific information and arguments from the reading. Basically, the professor wants you to a) make an argument, and b) show that you've done the reading for the class. This is pretty much standard when it comes to essay questions on college exams. No one wants to see you mindlessly regurgitate facts; that's what the short-answer section's for. Instead, you're supposed to synthesize; you're supposed to come up with some sort of thesis and develop it. At the same time, your essay should identify specific points from the reading assignments, to show both that you've kept up with the reading, and that you've *understood* it.

Problem-oriented exams
You'll encounter these exams in math or science courses. Sometimes, these tests are multiple-choice, but more often you'll be expected to answer a handful of longer problems. Some will be straightforward, and just require that you plug numbers into a formula, while others will ask you to apply your knowledge to a practical problem or situation.

Take-home exams
As the name suggests, you complete these exams at home, usually over a designated period of time. They're typically open-book, so you can

consult your course books and notes (but not other students). These tests involve the honor system; you're not supposed to exceed the allotted time (without informing your professor), or discuss the exam with anyone besides the instructor. Take-homes are nice because they take some of the pressure off; you don't have to memorize a lot of facts or figures and you usually have more than an hour or two to finish them. On the other hand, they're typically longer and more involved than in-class exams.

Oral exams

These are rare, but lethal. Just hope that they're not in front of the whole class. Your professor may ask you to memorize and recite a poem during office hours or during class, or may simply ask you several questions to which you must extemporaneously respond.

TEST-TAKING STRATEGIES

Excerpts from *50 Fun Things To Do In a Final That Does Not Matter,* a popular list circulated on the Internet.

- Bring cheerleaders.

- Walk in, get the exam, sit down. About five minutes into it, loudly say to the instructor, "I don't understand *any* of this. I've been to every lecture all semester long! What's the deal? And who the hell are you? Where's the regular guy?"

- Fifteen minutes into the exam, stand up, rip up all the papers into very small pieces, throw them into the air and yell out "Merry Christmas." If you're really daring, ask for another copy of the exam. Say you lost the first one. Repeat this process every fifteen minutes.

- As soon as the instructor hands you the exam, eat it.

- Every five minutes, stand up, collect all your things, move to another seat, continue with the exam.

- Try to get people in the room to do the wave.

- Get deliveries of candy, flowers, balloons, or telegrams sent to you every few minutes throughout the exam.

Chances are your exam *will*, in fact, matter, and if that's the case, here are some strategies that will help you once the blue books come out and the clock starts ticking.

Eat breakfast.

It does a body good. If your exam's in the morning, have breakfast before you get there. Taking 15 minutes to have a bagel or a glass of juice can make a huge difference in the way you feel during the exam. It'll keep you alert and save you the embarrassment and distraction of a loudly growling stomach during the exam.

Glance through the test before you begin.

Look over the exam quickly to see how many sections there are, how much each part is worth, and how long each one will take you. Scan the questions, especially essay questions, and try to do the easiest ones first.

Watch the clock.

No matter what kind of test you're taking, you need to keep a close eye on the clock. For instance, if you're taking some kind of short-answer exam and you get hung up on one, move on. They're all worth the same anyway, and why waste time on number 21 if number 22 is cake? Similarly, if you're taking a two-hour exam consisting of two equally weighted essay questions, don't let yourself spend an hour and a half on the first one. Also, allow yourself ten minutes or so at the beginning of each long essay to quickly sketch the flow of your argument. It'll save you time in the long run and make for a much more coherent, persuasive essay.

Fight tooth and nail for every point.

Even if you can't completely figure out a problem, even if you can only remember the book a quote came from, and not who said it, write it down. You'll get at least partial credit. Few people get everything perfect; just showing that you have a grasp of what the question is asking, that you know what direction you're going in, can take you a long way.

When in doubt, guess.

Obviously, you should guess on multiple-choice or true-false exams; your chances of guessing right range from one in four to fifty-fifty. Not bad odds. But you should, as a rule, take educated guesses on as many questions as you can; it's far better than leaving anything blank, and again, you'll give yourself a shot at some partial credit.

Name-drop shamelessly.
Pack your test with all the substantially relevant facts—names, dates, theories—you can remember. Don't forget to cite the reading or lectures the information came from. And include catchphrases. Certain phrases or word combinations that came up in readings or lectures will catch the T.A.'s or professor's attention, and hopefully make you seem more knowledgeable than you actually are.

Proofread your work.
By the time you're done with your exam, your wrist is probably aching as much as your head. The last thing you want to do is look it over. But if you have enough time, it definitely pays to glance quickly through your blue book(s). Make sure you didn't miss a page. Make sure you answered every short-answer question and picked up as many partial credit points as possible. Proofread your essays and make sure they have transition sentences. And please, please, please make sure you put your name on it.

If you're cracking the spines of your textbook the night before the exam, you have a lot to be nervous about, of course; obviously, you want to avoid that situation. Whatever you do, though, remain calm, both during the study process (however condensed), and during the exam itself. You'll retain and recall information a lot better when you're not completely freaked out.

WRITING PAPERS

Getting your first college paper back marked and graded may well be one of the biggest shocks of your academic career. In college, a five-paragraph essay consisting of an introduction, three supporting examples, and a conclusion that basically rehashes the introduction just doesn't cut it. You'll be expected to think, write, and argue critically at a much higher level in college than in high school, and it usually takes a few tries before you get it right.

GETTING STARTED: RESEARCH

If you're writing a literary essay, there's probably no need to consult secondary sources; in fact, many English and literature professors discourage reading outside criticism because it may influence or bias your interpretation of the text. If you're writing a paper for virtually any other subject, however, you're going to have to do some research. It's time to hit the library.

You can start off by searching your school's (hopefully) computerized card catalog to find relevant materials. Start your research early, because if other people are working on the same assignment, you may not find the resources you need. You may also have to check an actual card catalog to locate materials that were cataloged before the system became computerized. If you're writing on some sort of current issue, don't forget to check periodicals and microfiche. Your friendly neighborhood librarian can help you with your searches.

If you go to a university with graduate or professional schools, don't hesitate to raid their libraries and archives for information. Law libraries can be great for papers on politics, sociology, or international relations, and medical schools have lots of journals that might be helpful if you're writing on health or medical issues.

The Internet

Used properly, the Internet can save scores of hours of research time. Unfortunately, it also can also waste scores of hours of research time. If you can manage to avoid getting sidetracked to the *Seinfeld* home page for hours on end, the Web can be a great research tool. Did you wait until the last minute to start that paper? Is the library closed? Foolish, yes, but you need not abandon hope—the Web may be your savior yet, especially for political science or sociology papers that require information on current events.

First and foremost, the Net is a great place to find government documents and statistics. For instance, census data is available via the World Wide Web from the Department of Commerce Web site. You can find out details about a Department of Housing and Urban Development housing program at the HUD Web site, or see the latest demographic information on a foreign country at the Central Intelligence Agency Web site. The best way to get to what you want is through the White House, at www.whitehouse.gov. There, you can use the Interactive Citizen's Handbook to access the federal agency of your choice. For economics and business majors, financial information abounds on the Web—it's easy to get stock quotes and company profiles at sites like the Financial Times and CNN. Finally, most major news services, like CNN, MSNBC, the Associated Press, and the *Washington Post*, keep up a Web presence.

One word to the wise about research on the Web: Because it's so easy to put information out on the Internet, you may come across information that's distorted or simply wrong. Pay close attention to who is sponsoring the Web site you're using as a source. If you're getting a statistic from the State Department, you're probably fine. If you're getting statistics from the Foundation to stop the UN from invading Idaho, you might want to think twice.

Top Web Sites for Research

- Alta Vista: www.altavista.digital.com Alta Vista provides the ultimate site for finding things on the Net. Type in a word or phrase you want to find, and Alta Vista will search the full text of most of the Web.

- CNN Interactive: www.cnn.com Like its television brother, CNN provides the best place on the Net to get the latest news, weather, and sports.

- Library of Congress: www.loc.gov The Library of Congress Web site provides access to its directory of every book in existence. It also provides access to Thomas, a listing of legislative stuff.

- Microsoft: www.microsoft.com The Microsoft site provides everything you might ever need to know about your Microsoft Word software.

- Netscape: www.netscape.com It's lists of what's new and what's cool are a great place for first-time Web surfers to start. Also, its information on building your own Web page is outstanding.

- The White House: www.whitehouse.gov In itself, the White House site provides little beyond the expected political stuff. However, its Interactive Citizen's Handbook remains the best directory of government information on the Web.

- Yahoo: www.yahoo.com The virtual yellow pages of the Internet, Yahoo provides an organized index of most major web sites. The first place to go when looking for something.

- *Yale Daily News:* www.ydn.org The nation's best college newspaper, for free.

Besides the Web, there are other ways to access information through the Net. Many colleges, along with the Library of Congress, maintain their card catalogs electronically on the Internet. So, if you're looking for a book or manuscript that's not available at your college, you may be able to check other, nearby schools for the publication, and then either visit the other institution, or access the book via interlibrary loan.

If you're lucky, your school subscribes to an online news service, like Nexis. Nexis allows researchers to search a large body of newspapers, magazines, and public documents for a word or phrase. It can save literally thousands of hours of research time. Although Nexis usually goes back only about ten years, it is a great place to do research on a current events-type topic.

WRITING THE PAPER

You've made the photocopies, checked out the books, and surfed the Web. Time to roll up the sleeves and write your paper.

The thesis

We're not talking book report here. We're not talking five-paragraph essay. A college-level critical essay challenges you to formulate a concise yet powerful thesis, and argue it persuasively in a well-organized and well-written paper.

Essentially, your ultimate task in a college essay or paper is to make an argument. Sounds simple, we know, but in reality it's very different from the type of writing people do in high school. You're not summarizing plots or reporting facts; rather, you're using those facts and observations to support and argue a thesis, or a premise. For example, "In Homer's *Odyssey,* characters frequently withhold or conceal their identities" is an observation. On the other hand, "In Homer's *Odyssey,* the withholding or disguising of identity consistently appears as an effective strategy and means of asserting power in a relationship" is a thesis. The most powerful theses are usually surprisingly simple. If you can't explain the essence of what you're arguing in one concise sentence, you've got a problem.

The outline

Before you begin writing, try charting your course with an outline. It doesn't have to be detailed or formal; you just need a thumbnail sketch of your paper that clearly states your thesis and roughly plots the *movement* of your paper, how you're going to develop your argument. The outline should reflect the progression and development in your paper, should clearly show how you move from A to point B. It's impossible to produce a well-organized and logically argued paper without a clear idea of where you're going *before* you begin writing.

The moment of truth

The opening of your paper is what hooks your reader, so to speak, what intrigues him. You want an introduction that not only lays out what you plan to argue, but also draws your reader by piquing his curiosity and stirring his sensibilies. Not surprisingly, then, you may find the introduction a struggle to write. It's worth the time, though; writing a powerful opening sets up your whole essay, both on paper, and in your mind.

The body of your paper should, of course, develop the points you've chosen to bolster your argument. The structure of the paper will depend largely on whether you're comparing or contrasting, refuting a statement, or defending a policy. In all cases, though, you should include sufficient background, cite specific examples, and constantly evaluate the logic and flow of your argument. Make sure your points follow smoothly and logically from one another.

Your conclusion, like your introduction, should leave your reader with a powerful impression. Don't just reiterate your arguments; make your reader believe in them.

Citations

Your essay should include impeccably accurate and complete footnotes or endnotes, as well as a "Works Cited" page that lists any or all of, well, your works cited. For the appropriate style, check an *MLA* handbook or *The Chicago Manual of Style.*

You probably know that failure to properly attribute someone else's words amounts to plagiarism. But using someone else's *ideas* without giving them credit also constitutes plagiarism, and many schools are merciless about oversights. Even infractions as minor as putting the wrong page number on a footnote can draw investigation and disciplinary action. So do everything you can to avoid this academic no-no. When you're taking notes, be sure to *clearly distinguish* between what the source says and your own ideas or reactions. Your notes from source materials should be precise and detailed to avoid any sort of problems with attribution. When you are preparing your footnotes, include anything that is not obviously common knowledge; when in doubt, cite it. Be obsessively accurate. And whatever you do, never, never write your paper with the intention of putting in all the footnotes after you're done; it's a pain in the butt to later go searching for stuff you cited, and you're bound to miss something.

You're Stylin'

Never underestimate the importance of mechanics, style, and presentation; it can make a substantial difference in your grade. Check out authoritative references like *The Chicago Manual of Style* and Strunk and White's *Elements of Style* for specific points. Otherwise, the single most important thing you can do clean up your prose is *proofread* it. Neglecting this simple task can cost you big time in the grade department. Professors do not take kindly to misspelled words, incomplete sentences, and missing punctuation.

If you have time, take your paper to a writing tutor. Most schools hire writing tutors who meet with students by appointment, read their work, and offer constructive suggestions and advice. A writing tutor can help you add eloquence to your thoughts and style to your substance.

Good writing can't disguise substantive mediocrity, but it can transform a persuasive argument into a potent and affecting essay.

Drafts and Rewrites

One of the most important things you can do to write a good paper is discuss it with your professor or T.A. Show up at office hours or make an appointment to discuss your thesis and argument. If you're given the option to write a draft, take it. This takes a lot of discipline, but your final product will be immeasurably better. And if you're dissatisfied with your grade after you've gotten a paper back, ask if the teacher will accept a rewrite. Most professors and T.A.'s will be more than happy to let you rewrite the paper.

THE WONDERS OF TECHNOLOGY

You finish an essay and realize with a sinking heart that you're way over, or infinitely worse, way under, the suggested word count. As the clock ticks and your deadline nears, desperation sets in.

It's time to play with fonts.

> My computer has assisted me in many ways, including font acrobatics. It's amazing how changing a font from Times New Roman 12 point to, say, Arial 12 point can give that poor little 13-page paper the extra push it needs to reach its dream of 15 pages.
>
> —Junior, Harvard University

If your professor is clever and gives you a word count rather than a page length, or tells you specifically what font and margin size you should use, you're out of luck. If you're told simply to write a seven-page paper, you have a little more to work with.

A word of caution before you grab for the mouse: it's possible (OK, likely) that a professor will not be fooled by a computer-enhanced paper. T.A.'s, in particular, know all about fonts; they probably use Courier themselves on a fairly regular basis. There are ways to *subtly* expand or condense a paper that's slightly over or under specified length. But if the assignment was a term paper and you wrote a response paper, your options are quite limited.

If all else fails, here are a couple of subtle and not-so-subtle tricks to stretch or chop your masterpiece.

Use footnotes, not endnotes.
Footnotes go right into your text and take up lots of room. Conversely, use endnotes if you've gone too far over.

Center and block your quotes.
Technically, you're supposed to single-space quotes longer than two lines, but if you're desperate, go ahead and double space.

Play with the margins.
One-inch margins are fairly standard. Changing them to 1.1 inches all around is barely noticeable, and adds about a half-page to a seven-page essay. Friends in dire straits have been known to go as high as 1.25 inches around, but that tends to make text look like it's running in a column down the middle of your page. If you're over, you can't really make the margins any smaller than one inch.

Change the spacing.
If you're trying to shrink your paper, you can go as low as 1.5 spaces between lines without damaging your professor's eyesight. If you want to expand the paper, and your computer lets you, change the spacing to 2.1 lines. You'd be surprised how much you can add. You can also increase the spaces between your paragraphs.

Experiment with fonts.
There's an enormous range of fonts and sizes. A paper in Courier 12 point is nearly twice the size of the same essay in Times 10 point. So take some time out to explore the universe of fonts.

> Popular fonts, from smallest to largest. Higher number indicates a higher level of panic.
>
> 1. Times 10 point: About the lowest you can go without blinding your professor.
>
> 2. Times 12 point: The ideal font. Pat yourself on the back.
>
> 3. Palatino 10 point: About the same size as Times 12, but not as pretty.
>
> 4. Palatino 12 point: Perfectly acceptable.
>
> 5. New York 12: This font and size looks like it belongs in a Dr. Seuss Easy Reader.
>
> 6. Courier 12: Hideously ugly, but it does the job. It looks much smaller than the colossal New York 12, even though it's actually slightly larger.

THE PITFALLS OF TECHNOLOGY

Yes, your computer can expand or shrink your paper, bending it at your will. But it can do oh so much more.

> I had about an hour. After spending the last 36 hours—give or take a few breaks here and there—on a paper that I hoped would be, had to be, the best damn piece of writing I would ever produce, I was closing in on the final hour before it was due at the history department office. And it was at this moment I learned an invaluable lesson: Never let an electronic appliance know you are in a hurry.

Just moments after I hit the print button and waited for the paper to start feeding into the machine, nothing happened. I waited some more and still, nothing happened. My printer, for all intents and purposes, had deserted me. It was broken.

I didn't really panic because I knew I could easily print at the library and still had an hour, but I hadn't slept in quite some time and couldn't help but be a bit annoyed. I quickly saved my paper onto a disk and headed out the door. The library wasn't crowded and I had no trouble finding an open computer. But it could have been disaster.

—Junior, Northwestern University

How do they know? How do they know to lose a file, erase your paper, or run out of ink at precisely the worst moment they could possibly do so? The question is futile to ask, kind of like asking where the other sock goes when you do laundry. The only thing you can do is take these measures to protect your masterpiece:

Always remember to save your work.
Often. Most modern word processors have an "autosave" function, which will save a document every ten or 20 minutes. Figure out where yours is and activate it.

Know what you're doing (sort of).
Most good word processors have a help choice prominently displayed on the menu. Explore this feature as soon as you start using the word processor, as it can save you a lot of hassle. More importantly, skim the manual for the software to find out what kind of features your program has and how to avoid or fix various meltdowns and disasters.

Leave extra time for printing.
If you don't have your own printer, you need to leave time to go to the public cluster and print your work. If you do have your own printer, something is bound to go wrong if you're working at the last minute. If the paper is due at 5 P.M., try to print in the early afternoon. That way, you will have plenty of time in case the cluster is crowded, your printer cartridge runs out, or you find an ugly typo on page two.

Many new word processors also have handy features that will check your grammar and spelling, and let you look up synonyms in a thesaurus. Although these features are helpful, they are far from a panacea for lousy spelling and grammar. A spell checker does little more then take each word and match it to a word in the computer's built-in list. So if the computer doesn't have a word in its list, even if it's spelled correctly, it'll flag the word as being misspelled. Spell checkers almost never have proper nouns in them, so you'll be looking plenty of words up in the dictionary anyway.

As for grammar checkers, these handy devices will catch basic mistakes like overuse of the passive voice or using "too" for "to." But you'll get far more out of a quick perusal of Strunk and White's *Elements of Style* or a similar manual than out of your automatic grammar checkers. These checkers often flag outstanding style as bad; one found dozens of errors in Lincoln's Gettysburg Address.

AFTER HOURS

part **3**

WORKING AT SCHOOL

Unless you plan to beg, borrow, and steal your way through school, chances are you're going to have to find a job at some point in your college career. The search for legal and gainful campus employment can be a challenging one, but textbooks, course packets, and kegs do not buy themselves, my friend. There are jobs out there if you look early and hard enough.

Before you hit the pavement, you need to decide whether or not you really want a job your first semester freshman year. Between academics, activities, and meeting a slew of new people, taking a regular job might mean sacrificing some important aspects of your first year. You might want to wait until second semester freshman year to start looking for a job; a lot of campus jobs actually open up second term.

If you're a work-study student, there are probably several campus jobs designated as federal work-study jobs, meaning the government pays a percentage of your salary. As a work-study student, you probably need to have a regular term-time job first semester, so start looking as soon as you arrive on campus. Begin your job search late and you may end up serving vegan shepherd's pie in the dining halls. If your school has a student employment office, check it for job postings or listings. Your school may also have a World Wide Web site where campus employers can post job descriptions and wage or schedule information. Keep your eyes open for postings or announcements around campus, and follow them up with a phone call or visit promptly. Since most office and library jobs on campus don't require specialized skills, applicants often don't have to submit résumés, and are hired on the basis of an informal interview. Many employers fill spots on modified first-come, first-serve basis, so it's important to start your job-hunt early.

Your Options

Depending on how much money you need to contribute to your tuition, books and personal expenses, you'll have to figure out what kind of job best suits your needs. You may need a steady campus job with regular weekly hours. On the other hand, you may need only to give your cash flow the occasional jump start. Here are some of the most common types of campus jobs.

Steady Jobs

The library

Library jobs are good because the hours tend to be flexible; libraries usually hire a large number of students to cover the many hours that they're open, and you're bound to find hours that work into your schedule. Working in the library generally entails shelving books, manning the circulation desk, or keeping watch at the exits for deranged book thieves trying to slip Hegel down thier pants.

The office job

Administrative offices and academic departments often hire students to do clerical work such as typing, filing, and running errands. These jobs tend to be pretty menial, but if you don't mind papercuts and need to work a lot of hours, they're not too bad. If you are applying for office jobs, keep your eye out for interesting prospects like the admissions office. Also, if you have computer skills and your office job requires extensive computer work, you may be eligible for a higher wage.

The lab job

If you're interested in the sciences or just like cutting up rats, the lab may be the place for you. Chemistry, biology, and physics professors often hire undergraduates to help with their research. Don't get too excited; you won't be splicing DNA. But washing test tubes can be very rewarding. There is a plus side to lab jobs, though—eventually you probably *will* get to contribute to interesting research. And working for a professor in a lab job can open up opportunities for summer research or future academic projects. Most technical lab jobs are paid; if you're doing more advanced work, you might receive school credit instead.

Other research jobs

Professors in all fields, but particularly the social sciences, are always looking for slaves to help search archives, dig up statistics, or proofread drafts. As with the lab job, your work will probably be more menial than groundbreaking, but you will make connections, get experience in the research process, and pad your résumé. Again, some research jobs yield course credit rather than good old-fashioned cash.

The dining hall

Dining hall jobs are not the most coveted of campus job opportunities, but serving turkey teriyaki has its privileges. Schedules are usually pretty flexible, and you'll obviously be working during meal times, which means you're not cutting into study or social time. Also, if your campus's service workers are unionized, your wages may be higher than those of students at other campus jobs. On the down side, you might not want to eat in the dining halls once you've seen the inside of the juice machines.

> Dining hall work is great. You get decent pay, and three hours of light manual labor is not bad at all. It's one of the best-paying jobs on campus.
>
> —Sophomore, Yale University

Campus computing

Some schools hire students to work as computing assistants. As a C.A., you may have to provide computer support to the incompetent masses at public computer clusters, or even make housecalls. If you know HTML and are a self-starter, you might be able to work independently designing home pages for various academic departments. These jobs usually pay big money, so if you have the skills, go for it.

Local jobs

Local stores and restaurants surrounding campus sometimes hire students. While you may find a really fantastic place to work, off-campus employers are often not as understanding about your academic schedule, and might not pay as much as on-campus jobs. It's also not a good idea to take a job too far from campus; you don't want to be paying an arm and a leg in transportation costs or losing an arm or a leg after walking home from work through a sketchy neighborhood.

> The city has so many preprofessional opportunities and such good public transportation, it just made a lot more sense to look for a job off campus. I've worked with public interest organizations and in law offices, seen the inside of a courtroom and judges' chambers, and gotten paid a lot more than I did at my on-campus job.
>
> —Senior, New York University

Quick Cash, Low Commitment

Babysitting
Professors have kids too, and those kids need their diapers changed. Sure, it's not the most glam job in the world, but it does mean fast cash and minimal commitment.

Escort services
Oh, come on. Get your mind out of the gutter. We're talking student escort services here. Some schools hire students, usually on a floating or rotating basis, to walk a student patrol and respond to calls for campus escorts after dark. These jobs offer pretty good money for just one evening of cruising campus in an ugly orange vest.

Tutoring
Find out if your school has paid peer tutoring programs. If you have special expertise in some subject, you may be able to keep a classmate's grades out of the crapper while lining your wallet.

Grading papers
If you speak a foreign language fluently, you might be able to get a job grading papers, quizzes, or exams for introductory classes in that department.

Reunions and other functions

Your school may hire undergraduates to serve or bartend at alumni events or social functions.

Experiments

OK, it's not exactly a job, but it's a fast and easy way to earn money. Psychology students and professors can pay you up to $20 an hour to analyze inkblots with minielectrodes attached to your face. One warning: If you go to a university with a medical school or research hospital, steer clear of the physiological and medical experiments that require you to submit to shady tests or procedures. Experiments to avoid include any that involve the terms *hallucinogen, biopsy,* or *PET scan.* Selling your body to science for thousands may sound fine in theory, but the phrase *perfectly safe experimental drug* sounds vaguely sinister. And why the five-page release form?

NONTRADITIONAL CAMPUS JOBS

- Tour guide—Tell lies to prospective students.
- Nude modeling for the art department—Take it all off, and get immortalized in a work of art.
- The athletic department—many of these jobs require you to "monitor" the weight room or distribute towels to extremely buff and sweaty people.
- Publication gatherer—Wander around campus and collect student publications for the University library.
- Psych experiments—Unlike the old days, when college students were sometimes traumatized by weird psychology experiments, student psych experiments are usually regulated and often are a good source of easy money.

THE BALANCING ACT

If you've managed to find a job in which you make your own hours or work from home, you should have no trouble scheduling work time at convenient hours, such as between classes or in the early afternoon. You will, however, have to be more disciplined than if you had a job with regularly scheduled hours. If you work in some obscure library or office, you might be able to study on the job. But in most cases, you'll be forced to maintain a precarious balance between your campus job, schoolwork, friends, and extracurriculars.

The first thing you should do is figure out what your best study times are—when you're most productive—and try to leave some of those hours free. For example, if you tend to get a lot of studying done in the chunk of time between classes and dinner, don't break up your afternoons; instead look for jobs that require you to work in the mornings.

Second, always let your employer know what your needs are. If you have three midterms and a paper in one week, let your boss know, in advance, that you may need to limit your hours or even take some time off. Also, if you feel your job is placing unreasonable demands on your time, let your boss know right away; she may not realize how taxing or how time-consuming the work is. Most campus employers realize that you're a student first, and if yours doesn't, it might be time to leave.

Above all, recognize that you might not be able to do it all, especially as a freshman who's constantly meeting new people and adjusting to a whole different lifestyle. So make an effort to study more efficiently, communicate with your employer, and work in time to socialize. But if you do become overwhelmed, realize that something (besides sleep) is going to have to get the shaft, and if it's at all financially feasible, your job should be the first to go.

SUMMER JOBS AND INTERNSHIPS

If you've already landed an interesting term-time research job or comparable employment that pays fairly well, find out if you can stay on through the summer—you'll save yourself the work and anxiety that invariably accompanies the summer job search. Otherwise, you need to start hunting early for summer employment. Internship deadlines vary widely, but you should definitely begin surveying your options before Thanksgiving break.

Before you start applying, consider what your goals are for the summer. If you want to spend time overseas, look for programs that let you teach English or SAT preparation to high school students abroad, or work as a nanny for a foreign family. If you need to make money, the usual suspects include waiting/waitressing, sales, and office work. If making money to help with tuition or saving for books or travel is not a necessity, you widen your options considerably. Newspapers, science labs, nonprofit organizations, corporations, and government agencies that don't offer paid summer positions may take unpaid interns. It's free, back-breaking labor for them, and preprofessional, résumé-padding experience for you.

> During my summer internship on Wall Street, students were wandering around in business suits like Mr. or Ms. Junior Executive. It was very easy to get sucked into this feeling that you're very important—that you are a master of the universe, straight out of *Bonfire of the Vanities,* that you can rescue failing Latin American economies, merge one major health care concern with another, and underwrite a major bond offering—and that's all before lunch.
>
> —Recent graduate, Harvard University

Where to Start

There are, of course, jobs that both give you valuable preprofessional experience and a decent wage, but it takes a considerable amount of time, effort, and planning to snare one.

- Begin at your college or university's office of career services; they receive job announcements from all types of organizations and hopefully maintain updated, accurate files on a host of different programs. Also, search your career center's library for books on internship programs at home and abroad.

- Hit the Internet. If you're interested in nonprofit organization or government agencies, many have internship information (and even downloadable applications) on their home pages.

- Check the classified ads in local newspapers for job postings or announcements.

- As you wander campus and the streets, keep your eyes open for Help Wanted signs in front of stores and restaurants, or job announcements posted by professors or departments.

- Milk connections shamelessly. Ask older students about jobs they've held previously, or take advantage of your school's alumni network. A phone call or letter to an alum might not yield results, but there's really no harm in trying. And as you begin to scrape the bottom of the barrel, there's always nepotism; don't hesitate to enlist the help of parents and family members in your quest for employment.

- If you're looking for a science lab job for the summer, try your campus' science departments or medical school first. Professors are usually tripping over themselves to hire competent students to mix their chemicals and kill their bunnies. If you can't find anything at your own school, try hospitals, medical centers, or other universities. You can enlist the help of your school's science departments to find suitable employment elsewhere, or you can read journal articles and independently contact the professors or researchers that author them.

APPLYING YOURSELF

The application process for most jobs involves designing a résumé that will seduce employers, composing a cover letter or letter of interest that won't find its way into the wastepaper basket, and nailing an interview. Your school's career services center should offer regular workshops on résumé- and letter-writing, and even practice interviews. Take advantage of all these programs; a polished résumé and impressive interview can mean the difference between the internship of your dreams and spending the summer mowing lawns.

The Résumé

Your résumé is essentially a concise summary of your education, significant work experience, extracurricular activities, awards, skills, and interests. It should also include your full name, as well as permanent and term-time addresses and phone numbers. For college students, and really anyone who has been out in the work force for fewer than five years, a resume shouldn't exceed more than one typed page, and no entry should run longer than three or four lines.

The person who reads your résumé will probably have a slew of others crossing his desk at any given time. That's why it's so important that yours grabs his attention. Include your title, if you had one, or make one up if you didn't. When describing your work experience, use action verbs like *implemented*, *designed*, or *coordinated*. Highlight any impressive awards or achievements, as well as valuable skills like knowledge of a foreign language or computer proficiency. You should list and briefly describe all significant jobs or extracurricular activities you've held, along with your title, any leadership positions, and the dates you were employed, beginning with the most recent.

Prospective employers will consider your résumé a writing sample, so keep it concise, to-the-point, and, above all, proofread. A typo on your résumé is like a knife to the jugular.

And finally, when it comes to a résumé, presentation is everything. You definitely don't need fancy, monogrammed paper, but you do want a résumé that's neat and visually appealing. Keep it simple; don't use distracting fonts or overuse boldface or italics. As a final option, you can get computer software to design a résumé, or follow the format that your school's career office recommends.

The Cover Letter

When you send your résumé out to prospective employers, you normally enclose a cover letter or letter of interest with it. Like the résumé, your cover letter is considered a writing sample. Keep the letter concise (less than a page) and its language precise. Finally, although it's a formal letter, let your voice come through. Humor, enthusiasm, and personality in your letter can only help you.

Your letter should include where you learned of the job opening, if someone who's connected with the organization referred you. Tailor your cover letter to the job; highlight relevant on-the-job experience or coursework, explain how your interest in this job and its general field developed, and write frankly about your future career aspirations. Don't be afraid to repeat information that appears in your résumé.

References

You don't need to send prospective employers recommendations or the names or addresses of references unless they ask. Obviously, list only those former employers or professors with whom you've had good relationships as references, and check with them before you list them. If you do need to solicit a letter of recommendation for a job or program, ask your former boss or professor far in advance. Schedule a phone or in-person conversation with your recommender to discuss the job or internship for which you're applying. You'll also want to provide the recommender with a copy of résumé to look over and an addressed, stamped envelope to in which to mail the recommendation.

The Interview

If you get past the résumé/cover letter stage, an employer may invite you for a personal interview or request a phone interview. The employer has read a summary of your experience and accomplishments; the interview is a chance to flesh out that information and wow your interviewer with your poise and personality. Prepare to answer questions about your background and experiences, your interests, and your career goals. You might also get a hypothetical question thrown at you, something about how you'd handle a certain workplace situation or go about tackling a specific project. Rehearse the interview and try to anticipate specific questions before you walk in the door. Preparing beforehand will make you less nervous and more articulate during the actual interview. Here are some other tips to keep you from blowing it.

- Arrive on time. Showing up late destroys your interview before it's even begun.

- Dress neatly and conservatively. The type of job for which you're interviewing will dictate how formal your dress should be, but men should generally wear a jacket and women a nice blouse with a conservative skirt or slacks. Wearing a miniskirt or too much makeup can harm your chances. Especially if you're a guy.

- Don't chew gum, twirl your hair, shift in your seat, or fidget during your interview.

- Without overdoing it, maintain eye contact with your interviewer, lean slightly forward in your seat, and nod attentively from time to time. It makes you seem earnest and interested.

- At the end of the interview, your interviewer will invariably ask you if you have any questions about the job or the organization. Prepare a couple of questions beforehand that show you've done a little research. And don't let your salary be the first inquiry that escapes your lips.

- When your time's up, thank your interviewer politely for her time. It's OK to ask when you can expect to receive a decision. But don't harass your interviewer after the fact; allow plenty of time before you call to find out if she's made a decision.

- Follow your interview up with a short, polite, and sincere thank-you note. No butt kissing.

Both campus jobs and internships can give you valuable work experience, not to mention the income you need to get through the semester. Keep in mind, though, that both involve a considerable time investment. If you can afford it, it's probably a good idea to hold off on the job search, at least until second semester freshman year. After that, wash as many test tubes or bus as many tables as your budget requires.

12 EXTRACURRICULAR ACTIVITIES

When I was applying to colleges I had a conversation with a friend's father. His one piece of advice that I have taken very much to heart about how to do well in college is this: If you want something, go out and get it because no one is going to bring it to you. He is right. There are thousands of opportunities available at college. From ethnic clubs to PIRGs, from student government to a cappella groups, it is simply a matter of getting up and going for it. But while it seems like such simple advice, it is one of those things that is much easier said than done. Doors only open when you knock on them. If you're waiting for someone to open the door for you, you may be waiting a long time.

—Junior, Trinity College (Conn.)

During your first week at college, every campus organization under the sun from the school newspaper to the coed inner tube water polo team will be wooing you, competing for your attention and persuading you to join their ranks. Some schools have literally hundreds of student organizations, and in the face of this dizzying array of opportunities you'll probably find yourself signing up for activities you never knew existed. Seize this opportunity; your freshman year of college is your chance to pursue interests you've already developed as well as try out things you've never even considered before.

Why Join?

Activities can be the single fastest way to meet people who live outside your dorm and share interests similar to yours. As a freshman, your social circle is initially limited to the people who live on your floor or hallway. You can rapidly expand that circle by getting involved in extracurricular organizations, which are often serious bonding venues; at the very least let you meet hordes of other freshmen.

An extracurricular activity also provides vitally necessary downtime. Playing an intramural football game, practicing your Italian at a language table, or playing the violin with the orchestra can all give you a much-needed break away from studying, writing papers, or a campus job. Getting involved in the right activity can round out your first-year experience and add some variety to your life.

Extracurricular activities also look great on your résumé. Employers and graduate schools will want to see that you have interests and have devoted time to something outside of your academic work. Performing with a musical or theatre troupe, writing for a campus publication, or competing with the debate team tell a graduate school or a prospective employer a lot. It shows that you are an interesting and well-rounded person, that you can manage your time efficiently, and that you have honed talents and developed valuable skills and experience.

Types of Activities

Chances are your campus will offer an enormous variety of activities, many of them obscure or bizarre. Here are some of the most common.

Publications

If writing's your thing, consider reporting for your campus newspaper or contributing to a literary magazine. There are usually so many publications, and so many different types, that you can find just about anything to suit your interest and the amount of time you're willing to commit. Contributing to publications lets you both improve your writing and collect published clips of your work that you can later use as writing samples.

Singing groups

Most campuses have glee clubs or choirs, some coed and others all-male or all-female. Your school may also have smaller a cappella singing groups. Usually, you have to audition to become a member of one of these groups, but don't be discouraged if you have no formal musical training. The time commitment for many of these groups might be considerable; typically, you'll be expected to attend a rehearsal or two each week and several concerts during the term. Members of these groups sometimes get to travel to other schools, concert halls, or even overseas to perform.

Concert band, marching band, or orchestra

Again, you almost certainly have to audition to join these groups, but don't underestimate your talent or overestimate their standards.

Drama

If you're an aspiring thespian, you can join a formal dramatic association or a small performance troupe. There also may be ample opportunity on your campus to write, direct, or produce your own shows.

Campus radio

Most campuses have their own student-run radio station and many now have their own television station as well. You may be able to work on programming, write or produce your own segments, DJ, or host a racy late-night call-in show.

> I'm a DJ at the radio station . It's very cool, even though I have the bastard time slot—2–5 A.M. You basically have to take the bastard slot some time or another; you have to pay your dues before you can get a good slot. For now, I go in every week for three hours, sit on my butt and play a lot of cool music. And, the best part is, I get to say stupid stuff over the air.
>
> —Junior, Duke University

Student government

Most campuses elect student representatives to some kind of official council. Each class may elect representatives, so you can choose to run specifically for a freshman class office.

Debate or mock trial

These groups may require tryouts, but again, don't hesitate to show up if you're interested, even if you had no high school debate experience. If you love to compete, are interested in going to law school or into politics, or just like to hear yourself talk, this may be the place for you.

Language clubs

Students with widely differing levels of proficiency meet to practice conversing in languages ranging from French to Yoruba. Language clubs sometimes also publish foreign language literary magazines, host screenings of foreign films, or sponsor theme dinners.

Preprofessional societies

Some schools have premed, prelaw, or preengineering societies. These are not exactly fun-packed organizations, but they serve some purposes; they're designed primarily to pad your résumé and let you start checking out the competition early.

Political organizations

If you have strong political leanings or want to get involved in campaigns on a good election year, you might want to join your school's College Democrats or College Republicans Club. As a member, you might sponsor drives to register voters, distribute literature, invite speakers, or participate in political debates or forums. In addition, most schools have a whole host of (technically) nonpartisan political and activist groups you can join, from the ACLU to pro-life organizations.

Cultural or religious groups

Again, you can find an enormous range on virtually any campus. These groups often sponsor cultural or religious events and forums, or just provide a place for students to meet, talk, or socialize. One warning: Be wary of religious groups that recruit a little too zealously or pressure you to attend meetings. Increasingly, college campuses are seeing the presence of cults (yes, cults), whose members target incoming freshmen. Students who get sucked into cultlike groups often spend most of their time at meetings, withdraw from regular campus life, drop friends and family, and let their academics slide. If you're feeling harassed or pressured or are watching a friend get deeply involved in an escalating situation, seek outside help from someone like an R.A. or counselor.

Community service

There are probably countless opportunities for service in the neighborhoods surrounding your school, particularly if you live in an urban area. You can volunteer at soup kitchens, women's shelters, or hospitals, deliver hot meals to AIDS patients, tutor children at local schools, or translate Spanish at a city legal aid society. Community service is also a great place to be a self-starter; if you see a need in the community that's not being met, you can probably find and organize a group of people that agree with you.

Intramural sports

Virtually every campus has some sort of intramural sports program. You don't have to be able to land a vault on one foot to participate; athletic prowess or natural ability is not a requirement. Basically, intramurals let you get up off your butt and do something physical and fun. Most campuses have intramural teams in everything from football to golf to Ultimate Frisbee.

Varsity and club sports

Varsity sports obviously mean a greater time commitment than the average activity. Many teams practice at least once and sometimes twice a day, and during the season, there might be meets or games every weekend. If you're interested in joining a varsity sport for which you were not recruited, by all means contact the coach when you get to school and attend tryouts. Keep in mind, though, that college-level athletic play, as compared with high school sports, is a whole different ball game, so to speak. Even though you were the star of you high school's cross-country team, you won't necessarily excel on, or even make, your college team. Club teams often practice as often as varsity teams, and have frequent intercollegiate teams or matches, but don't receive the official and financial supports that varsity teams do.

THE OVERCOMMITMENT BLUES

Although you'll probably attend many, many introductory meetings and sign up for many, many organizations in your first weeks, you'll soon find that college activities are really different from high school activities in that they involve a much deeper level of commitment. In high school, you might have simultaneously been captain of your swim team, editor of the school newspaper, and president of the art club without ever breaking a sweat, but most college activities typically entail more than a one-hour meeting once a week.

You'll find that academics and your social life take up a lot more time than they did in high school, and the activities themselves are far more intense. Producing a play or traveling with a debate association can take a large chunk out of your time. Leadership positions are also a lot harder to come by in college organizations, and if you want to rise through the ranks of most groups, you have to put in a fair number of hours.

Most students end up devoting most of their time to a single, intense extracurricular organization, while participating occasionally in activities that require less steady commitment, like intramurals or language clubs. You should definitely spend a lot of your first year experimenting and discovering groups of people and activities that are really you. Avoid overcommitting yourself, though; getting too involved as a freshman can introduce stress rather than relieve it. Try not to accept too many responsibilities that you'll have trouble getting out of later on; you wouldn't want to sacrifice study, party, or sleep time because you took on too much.

GREEK LIFE **13**

Generally speaking, the prevalence of Greek living, especially the *Animal House* variety, is down at most colleges and universities after taking a beating for widely publicized hazing practices—abusive treatment of pledges by active members. However, at some schools, particularly in the South, fraternities and sororities are still going strong.

Depending on your school, going Greek can be just another extracurricular activity, or a major lifestyle choice. On your campus, a frat might be your only ticket to decent parties and comfortable living. Or maybe you go to a college whose Greek life is less pervasive, and membership in one of your school's three obscure, houseless frats would make you something of a curiosity. Your decision to rush depends largely on the prevalence and character of the frats and sororities at your college or university. Because the variation between schools is so great, we can give you only the general pros and cons of donning a toga.

HOUSING

When it comes to Greek housing, neither the Victorian, pillared sorority house nor the beer-can laden brothel you see in the movies is the norm. Frat houses at most colleges are generally run-of-the-mill, fairly large houses, often clustered on one block near campus known as *frat* or *Greek row*. Living space is usually limited; not all members get to live in the house, and space is usually allotted by some kind of seniority system. You might have to share a bedroom with one or several of your "siblings," and everyone's expected to contribute to regular household duties. Most houses have their own cooks, so food quality can vary significantly from standard dorm fare and between different houses.

It's definitely possible that living in a frat or sorority house will prove pricier than living on campus. Room and board costs can be comparable to the dorms, but you also have to consider dues, which can run up to several hundred dollars a year, as well as the burden of having to bankroll frequent parties and expensive social functions. There are exceptions, however, so don't automatically assume that going Greek will leave you destitute; on some campuses, Greek housing is the most affordable kind available.

Not every fraternity or sorority has its own house. Some are merely close-knit social groups whose members meet frequently but live in the dorms or in off-campus apartments. Members host social functions, work together in the community, and develop friendships as in other frats, but these groups usually demand less of a time commitment and allow a lot more freedom. Membership in an unhoused frat is more of an activity than a major lifestyle decision.

Pros and Cons: Does Membership Have its Privileges?

Don't make a decision to rush or not to rush based on unfair and probably false stereotypes; fraternity brothers are not necessarily beer-guzzling, stupid jocks, and sorority sisters are not necessarily exclusive, superficial snobs. Try not to make any premature judgments; you can end up missing out on a lifestyle and community you would have really enjoyed. So if you're at all inclined, go to a couple of rush events and see for yourself whether stepping into the Greek scene is for you. Greek life isn't for everyone — many of the aspects of frats and sororities that appeal to some students turn off others completely.

One of the most frequently cited reasons for joining a fraternity or sorority is the opportunity for close-knit friendships and bonding. Greek life affords you a ready-made and devoted circle of friends. Greeks often develop strong ties and bonds with their brothers or sisters that last long after graduation. Membership can provide you not only with lifetime friendships, but with future professional connections as well.

On the flip side, your brothers and sisters can become the *only* members of your social circle. Living in a frat house deprives you of the diversity of the dorms. Brothers or sisters in the same house, are, at least in some respects, a homogeneous population; members are selected because they possess some preferred quality or combination of qualities. In the dorms you don't pick what types of people you live with. This can cause problems occasionally, but it can also turn out to be one of the richest aspects of your education.

Even before classes start, you're already in a sorority—it's the thing here. You have ties with alumni afterwards, for jobs and for references. You have leadership opportunities, and that great all-girl organization.

As a freshman, I got a big sis, and she really has become my big sis. Three years later she's already out of college and she's still my best friend. I talk to her every day.

—Junior, Arkansas State University

Joining a frat or sorority, especially if you live in a house, undeniably kickstarts your social life; you are probably at the heart of the campus party scene. There's never a dearth of things to do or events to attend.

On the other hand, you're usually expected or at least urged to attend these parties and events, which means your social decisions are heavily influenced if not dictated by your fraternity or sorority. You have a lot less freedom to do what you please with your downtime, and this can be a real problem for people who don't like their schedules to be weighed down or regimented.

Again, what some students view as advantages to Greek life others consider disadvantages. So if there's a Greek presence on your campus and you think you'd like to join up, take your time checking out your options and making you decision.

IF YOU WANT TO JOIN: THE PROCESS

At some schools, you're required to pledge or commit to a specific fraternity or sorority even before you arrive. Other schools require you to submit a preregistration form with your housing materials. Usually, though, there's some kind of one- to two-week "rush" period soon after you arrive at school or the beginning of second semester. Rush is your opportunity to attend a throng of Greek events and get a taste for different houses and, notoriously, different beverages. You don't have to make any commitments; rush week is simply your chance to gauge the "personalities" of different frats and figure out if Greek life is for you. In most cases, men get to choose which frat houses they want to rush, while women usually go through a more formal process, attending social functions or rush events at all campus sororities before narrowing the field.

At the end of the rush process, you might receive a "bid," or an invitation to join a frat or sorority. If you reject a bid, you're free to accept a bid at another house or walk away from Greek life altogether. If you accept a bid, you have to go through a pledge period, which can last up to a semester, before you become a full-fledged member.

Pledge period activities vary too widely from school to school to describe in detail here. Some frats or sororities have clandestine traditions or secret initiation rites for pledges, and most require pledges to perform various duties for active brothers or sisters. Mild humiliation is generally part of the process, though most houses have cut down on hazing, or abusive treatment of pledges, in recent years. However, hazing still takes place on many campuses, though every school officially bans it and may impose severe penalties on houses that do it.

> I pledged for one night. I did pushups—that was it. You can just tell by looking at the people that are pledging that they aren't having a good time. The guys in our pledge class had bags under their eyes, they just looked totally exhausted.
>
> —Junior, Hope College

The important thing to remember about the Greek rush process is that you can always turn down a bid; you can always walk away. So if you have slightest inclination to sample Greek living, go ahead and rush, attend as many parties and events as you want. Even if you decide not to join or don't receive a bid, rushing a house is a great way to meet and bond with other freshmen.

Dealing with Rejection

The Greek thing reaches a peak about January, when everyone's pledging. Almost everyone gets a bid from a fraternity or sorority here. Every year someone's heart gets broken, but inevitably if they do end up pledging their second or their third choice, and they're happy with it after the hangover wears off.

—Junior, Emory University

It sucks, but it happens. Fraternities and sororities are by definition exclusive, so you'll have to prepare for the possibility that you won't get a bid from the house of your choice. You might end up (very happily) at your second-choice house, or, in the worst-case scenario, you might not get into a frat or sorority at all. Getting rejected from anything is painful, but when it happens in what is essentially a social situation in the first few weeks of your college experience, it can be difficult to deal with. Keep in mind that you're being judged on the basis of a (maximum) three-week-long, somewhat superficial process. It might not seem like it, but being selected or rejected doesn't really have all that much to do with you as a person.

One final note: Pretending to be someone else to get into a house will only make for problems later on when your brothers or sisters discover your real interests and preferences. If you have to develop a whole new persona to get into a particular frat or sorority, you're probably not a good match for that house.

DRINKING ON CAMPUS

From beer games, to blue stuff, to keg parties, booze will flow literally everywhere on your college's campus, despite the fact that three-quarters of the student body is underage and your school may have, or even (gasp!) enforce, strict liquor policies. College students are a resolute and tenacious group, though, not likely to be swayed by a little liquor law in their quest for inebriation. Go to any given party (especially if it's of the Greek variety) on any given Friday, and chances are you'll find obviously thirsty people getting liquored up on cheap, watered-down beer and unidentified purple liquids, as they hit on people they'd avoid if sober (the "beer goggle" effect) and watch roommates gag over a toilet seat. Sated and exhausted, they stumble home and collapse into bed sometime in the early morning, only to awaken a few hours later feeling like hell and swearing off alcohol forever. That night, they go out and do it all over again.

Whether this sounds like an incredibly fun or an intensely bizarre scenario to you, it's probably an unfamiliar one; for a lot of students, college is their first exposure to readily available alcohol. The super-availablity of liquor, combined with the total and relatively new freedom of life away from home, can tempt you to get a little carried away in your revelry. Chances are you're going to see, engage in, and probably really like drinking in college, but it's important that you drink on your own terms and drink responsibly.

So many kids go crazy frosh year because they're not under their parents' control. There are two types of people: Those that settle down and become "normal" again and those that never adjust to their new freedom, smoking up every day or binge drinking three days a week well into their upperclassmen years.

—Junior, Duke University

THE 21 THING

The drinking age is 21. The majority of college students are not 21. The majority of college students drink. Obviously, the drinking age is not an insurmountable obstacle on the road to oblivion. Most drinking among underclassmen takes place in people's rooms, off-campus apartments, or frat houses—and fraternity brothers will likely not ask you for a valid proof of age at the door. They'll probably hand you a beer instead.

If they did ask you for a valid proof of age, of course, you could not comply. We'd never suggest bribing your older sister for her driver's license, looking for your long-lost twin among the senior class, or obtaining an "international student ID." That might put ideas in your head.

Seriously, though, drinking probably is illegal for you if you're reading this book, and underage drinkers have been caught and faced the wrath of a cop or disciplinary committee. Penalties range from a slap on the wrist to an actual charge, which will not look great on your record when you're applying to law school three years down the line.

Drinking policies at Baylor are strict for undergraduates. If they catch you drinking on this campus, you get in trouble. A friend had to go to an alcohol awareness class because she was caught drinking on campus—and she wasn't even drunk at the time.

—Senior, Baylor College

If you're drinking at a frat party or in someone's room, the chances of being caught are pretty slim, though it has happened before. Closing your door and not stumbling to your R.A.'s room in a drunken stupor will minimize the odds of getting busted. Using a fake ID is riskier; most bouncers and cops can spot one pretty quickly, and won't hesitate to confiscate it. Usually, the only consequence you'll face is the burden of finding another ID, but keep in mind that you're running the risk of all kinds of nasty repercussions, including arrest.

Setting Limits

The only thing your parents will like less than hearing you're in jail for drinking is hearing that you're in the hospital for drinking. Binge drinking is really common in college, and more students than you think have ended up at health services or even dead because they had too much too fast. You need to know your own limits, and be able to tell yourself when you've had too much. Spewing chunks or passing out is a good indicator, but hopefully you'll cease consumption before you reach that point. A lot of factors play into how hammered you're going to get and how fast, including your body weight, how much food you have in your stomach, your natural tolerance, and how quickly you down your beverages. People tend to get really drunk (and, inevitably, really sick) when they don't realize how quickly they're drinking; you have a couple of shots, then have a couple of mixed drinks before the shots kick in, and by that point, you're not in any shape to figure out you're already drunk. Here are a couple of things that you should handle with care.

Drinking games

From "Asshole" to "Quarters" to "I Never . . .," drinking games are a unique college phenomenon. Drinking games are usually played with beer, since the huge amount of alcohol they involve necessitates dirt-cheap liquor. Beer gets you drunk just as surely as other drinks, though, so don't think you're safe from hurling or hangovers. Drinking games force you to drink a ton in a really short amount of time, and before you know it you're passed out on the card table and your drunken friends are periodically checking that you haven't choked on your own vomit.

Mixed drinks and mystery punch

Mixed drinks tend to get you drunk a lot faster than beer. They also taste good, which is exactly the danger—you don't realize how much alcohol is in them, so you drink rum and coke after rum and coke, as the slur in your speech becomes progressively worse. And then there's mystery punch—available in a rainbow of fruit flavors, it usually contains grain alcohol that you can't even taste, but can leave you sick as a dog if you're lucky and in the hospital if you're not. Apply the same standard you would when scoping for someone to hook up with—avoid anything you can't identify.

Hard liquor

Hard liquor—vodka, whisky, gin, etcetera—is harder to come by than other beverages in college, partially because it's so expensive to drink straight. Doing shots of hard liquor is one of the worst things you can do when it comes to drinking. It's too easy to do three, four, five shots in a row (all followed by beer chasers, of course); again, you can end up very sick *very* quickly.

AFTEREFFECTS

> If you hear the toilet flushing a lot on a Friday night, the person in the stall probably isn't going to the bathroom.
>
> — Senior, Yale University

"Beer before liquor, never been sicker; liquor before beer, you're in the clear." Hah. Let us say that again. Hah. It doesn't matter what order you drink it in; if you drink enough of it, you will feel the pain. Any of the above practices will, at best, make you sick or leave you hung over the next morning. If you drink beyond your limit, there's not too much you can do to avoid a hangover. You can lessen its severity by drinking tons and tons of water throughout the night, and by taking some aspirin or ibuprofin before you go to bed, and again when you wake up in the morning.

Even if you're not the one who's hammered out out of his mind, chances are there will be plenty of yakking or loss of consciousness around you. Overindulging in alcohol can have serious—even lethal—consequences. If you take an incredibly drunk person home and put them to bed, it's possible that she'll choke on her own vomit or die from alcohol poisoning; it happens far more frequently than you think. If you think a friend is dangerously drunk, if that person has been puking violently, is turning blue, dry heaving, or having trouble breathing, you need to call health services. No one is ever reprimanded for drinking when he calls for help for a seriously drunk friend. So don't be afraid to call authorities if you think someone is dangerously ill.

OTHER CONSEQUENCES

Freshman year, some people overestimate the importance of getting uncontrollably drunk at frat parties and allow themselves to be put in compromising situations. The freshman experience is to get blasted out of your mind. You get sick, it's something you gotta do, but can lead to things you may regret later.

During my freshman year, I had an unforgettable experience during bid night for my sorority, when all the pledges are supposed to get insanely drunk. I was the most intoxicated I've ever been. I was pushing people out of the way on the dance floor doing the YMCA, and I'm normally a reserved person. I still cringe when I hear the song.

—Junior, Duke University

Even if you don't drink enough to get physically sick, alcohol has other effects that can leave you anywhere from mildly humiliated to terrified about what you did the previous night. Alcohol lowers inhibitions; the next morning you may be treated to stories from your friends about how you danced naked on tables in front of everyone you know. Worse yet, you may find yourself in the room of someone you don't even recognize. Although college students tend to laugh about a lot of alcohol-related escapades later, many end up doing things they really regret. Drunken hookups are extremely common in college; you might hook up with someone you with whom you definitely wouldn't ordinarily, or you can move more quickly than you might were you sober. The best-case scenario resulting from one of these encounters is a forced "walk of shame" Sunday morning in Saturday night's clothes. At worst, you'll have to worry about the consequences of unprotected sex. Drunk students are less likely to use protection when having sex, and less likely to put on a condom correctly when they do use one.

One final warning about drinking—this should go unsaid, but let's say it anyway—don't drive when you've been drinking. Even if you don't mind not seeing graduation yourself, think about the friends in your car and the people on the roads.

POT AND OTHER DRUGS

Besides alcohol, pot is by far the second most popular substance on college campuses (we'll leave caffeine and nicotine out of this). Even if you think recreational drugs should be legalized, even if you don't believe that pot isn't any worse for you than alcohol, be warned that the consequences are probably worse if you get caught smoking. Schools tend not to turn a blind eye toward toward pot use the way they might toward drinking. And if your R.A. drops by, it's a lot easier to hide a beer bottle than the unmistakable fragrance of weed. He will probably confiscate your stash and promptly report you.

Harder drugs are far less prevalent on college campuses, though they do turn up occasionally. No playing around here—drug use can destroy every aspect of your college life, affect your record, and even kill you. So think twice about even casual use; if you've developed a dependency, look for help from a friend, your R.A., or a counselor.

DATING AND SEX

"Sex kills, so come to [insert school name] and live forever."

This slogan appears on many a college student's T-shirt at colleges and universities across the country. As hard up as college students believe themselves, though, the truth is, love, lust, and heartbreak are as much a part of the college landscape as overpriced textbooks and unidentifiable food. Whether it's a monogamous relationship or a one-night fling on your roommate's desk, love and sex are inscapable realities of college life.

And with them come a whole other set of inescapable realities, both emotional and physical. This sounds cheesy, but college really means a lot of firsts for a lot of people, from first loves to first times (hopefully, but not always in that order). The dating game, good and bad, can take up a whole lot more (or a whole lot less) of your time than you may want. But whatever your situation, knowing how to protect yourself has become its most crucial rule.

YOUR LONG-DISTANCE LOVE

No one can tell you what to do about a long-distance relationship with your high school love; it's up to you to follow your instincts and evaluate your own situation. It is fair to say, though, that many a college freshman has gone home for Thanksgiving break attached and returned a free agent; the lion's share of long-distance relationships don't make it through first semester, and it's the rare, rare few that survive four years.

Which is not to say, though, that you shouldn't try if that's what you both want, but recognize that the odds are against you. And that while you're spending countless phone hours sobbing with your high school sweetheart or sending alternately doting and devastated E-mails, your roommate is meeting someone, dating someone, or even licking someone's earlobe. It sounds callous, but the reality is that most long-distance relationships deprive you of the unique sexual and dating freedom of a college campus; no matter how paltry your school's dating scene is reputed to be, your opportunities to fall in love or just satiate your carnal impulses will never be greater.

If you do decide to continue your long-distance relationship, you need to make sure that you're doing it for the right reasons. Too many freshmen use a long-distance love as a security blanket; as everything in your world changes, it's easy to view your high school sweetheart as the one fixed point that remains. The idea of breaking it off can make you feel like you're standing at the edge of the high board looking down into an empty pool. Though the feeling's entirely natural, it's not enough to justify staying in a long-distance relationship. While it may be painful in the short run, in the long run breaking up might be the best alternative for both of you.

THE DATING GAME

College provides a freedom that most freshmen have never known before. There's no possibility of your parents coming home, your hookup location options are somewhat wider than a backseat, and you have anywhere from several hundred to several thousand new people spread out before you like some kind of human Sizzler buffet. Before you know it, the whole thing can start to look like something out of the Discovery channel.

If you become involved in a steady relationship at school, be forewarned that they can threaten to take over your life. College affords you the opportunity to spend every waking (and nonwaking) moment with your new love. It's easy to get wrapped up in each other, and as the sleepovers become more frequent, everything else in your life can can drop a notch on your list of priorities. No one can tell you how much time is too much time when it comes to your relationship, but if it's preventing you from studying, socializing with your other friends, or sleeping on a fairly regular basis, it might be time to set some ground rules.

STAYING SAFE

Whether you're in a monogamous relationship or not, chances are sex is going to become an issue sooner or later. The decision to have sex is a highly personal one; *bad* reasons to do it include that your partner is pressuring you (ask yourself if you'd still want to if the person weren't putting pressure on you); or that you feel you're the last virgin on your campus (actually, a large percentage of students on many campuses are virgins, for religious or moral reasons, or just because they haven't met the right person). Sex *can* be a great part of a committed relationship when both partners are ready for it. But if you do decide to have sex, you both need to discuss how to stay baby- and disease-free *beforehand*.

You'd have to be a juror on the O. J. Simpson trial to have not heard about the risks of unprotected sex nowadays. Of course, the only way to to ensure that you won't contract AIDS or another STD (sexually transmitted disease) is by not having sex (or engaging in other high-risk behaviors). If you do decide to have sex, though, use of a latex condom, together with a lubricant containing Nonoxynol-9, can make it safer. If you and your partner have both tested negative for HIV and other STDs in the last six months, and are in a monogamous relationship, contraceptive methods besides a condom and spermicide may be an option. But no other method protects you against AIDS, and you really never know. Is your life really something you want to gamble with?

What follows are ways to prevent both pregnancy and getting a host of STDs that range from mildly annoying to lethal.

BIRTH CONTROL

Hormonal contraceptive methods, which include the pill, and newer options like Norplant and Depo-Provera, involve the use of synthetic female hormones to prevent ovulation and thus prevent pregnancy. Barrier methods like the condom, the diaphragm, and the cervical cap keep sperm from making its way into the uterus, and are often used (and are more effective) in conjunction with a spermicide. Spermicidal foams, creams, or jellies contain chemicals that kill sperm, and may reduce the risk of infection by various sexually transmitted bacteria or viruses, including HIV. The *only effective* contraceptive method that also protects you against contracting STDs is a latex condom with spermicide.

Hormonal Contraceptive Methods

The Pill (Oral Contraceptives)—97–98 percent effective

What it is: Combination birth control pills, the most commonly prescribed contraceptives, contain synthetic estrogen and progesterone, female hormones. The minipill, which is slightly less effective, contains only progesterone. Both elevate the level of estrogen in the body to prevent ovulation, and keep the uterine lining from becoming thick enough for an egg to implant.

Pros: The pill is a highly effective method of birth control; combination pills are 98 percent effective, while the progesterone-only minipill is 97 percent effective. Taking the pill also results in a lighter, more regular period, and may ease menstrual cramps and symptoms of PMS. The pill is also easy to get at most campus health clinics (by prescription only) at a far lower cost than in the real world; in fact, some college women say they try to stock up before graduation. Finally, the pill is a nonintrusive method of birth control; in other words, it doesn't interrupt your lovin'.

Cons: You have to take it *every* day, at the *same time,* without fail. If you have trouble remembering to take your keys with you when you leave your room every morning, this could present a serious problem. Missing a pill or two significantly reduces its effectiveness. The pill can cause some minor side effects that mimic the early signs of pregnancy, including nausea, breast tenderness, and water retention, but these usually subside after the first three months of use. If you smoke, the pill is not an option for you; major complications can occur, including high blood pressure and blood clots. Finally, the pill provides *no* protection against AIDS and other sexually transmitted diseases whatsoever. You should always use a condom as a backup.

FACTS ABOUT THE "MORNING-AFTER PILL"

The morning-after pill is actually an unusually high dosage of the synthetic hormones in birth control pills. When taken within 72 hours of sex, the pill is very effective in preventing an embryo from implanting in the uterine wall, thus preventing pregnancy. Side effects can include severe nausea, abdominal cramps, or vomiting.

It's very likely that you can obtain a morning-after pill at your campus' infirmary after speaking with a doctor or nurse practitioner. If you've had unprotected sex, or if the condom broke during sex, this may be an option you want to consider. The morning-after pill is not a quick fix, though, and it's not a substitute for appropriate birth control (i.e., condoms, which also prevent the spread of STDs); there can be negative side effects if you use it more than once in your lifetime.

Norplant—99 percent effective
What it is: A doctor inserts six thin, silicone capsules into your upper arm that continually release synthetic progesterone into your system. The hormone prevents ovulation, just as do birth control pills. You leave Norplant in for up to five years, after which time the capsules must be removed by a doctor.

Pros: Norplant is even more effective that the pill in preventing pregnancy, partly because there's no human (your) error involved; you don't ever have to worry about missing a dose.

Cons: Norplant's side effects are the same as with oral contraceptives—nausea, weight gain, tender breasts—but these usually subside after the first three months. You probably can't get Norplant implanted at your campus' health services, but they can refer you to a nearby Planned Parenthood or other clinic. You'll end up paying considerably more than you would with the pill; probably $500–$600. And finally, Norplant provides no protection against AIDS or other STDs, which means you'll still need to use a condom every time you have sex.

Depo-Provera—99 percent effective
What it is: Depo-Provera, like Norplant, is synthetic progesterone that prevents pregnancy by inhibiting ovulation. You get a needle in your arm or butt cheek once every three months.

Pros: Like Norplant, this is highly effective form of birth control that you don't have to worry about on a daily basis.

Cons: Side effects, restrictions, and possible major complications are the same as with the pill and Norplant. In addition, when you're done taking

Depo-Provera, it may take up to a year to regain fertility. As with Norplant, you may have to stray beyond your campus walls to find Depo-Provera and lay out a hefty chunk of change to get it, since it requires an exam and shot every three months. And last but not least, the shot doesn't protect you against AIDS and other STDs, so if you're having sex, bring on the latex. Are you beginning to detect a trend yet?

Barrier Methods

The Condom—90 percent effective

What it is: Condoms are currently the only (nonsurgical) method of birth control for men. The vast majority of condoms on the market now (and the ones you should look for) are of the latex variety. You can buy prelubricated condoms with Nonoxynol-9; lubrication cuts down on the risk of breakage, and the spermicide gives you added protection against both pregnancy and transmission of HIV.

Pros: Condoms are cheap, and they're accessible; you can get them in any drugstore, or campus pharmacy, and most dorms have a condom machine lurking in some discreet corner somewhere. Most important, use of a condom plays a crucial role in safer sex—a latex condom helps protect you against STDs, including AIDS.

Cons: Since you have to put on condoms immediately before sex, couples can find them distracting or annoying to use. Condoms also reduce sensation for men. Either the man or woman can have an allergic reaction to using condoms; in most cases, it's a reaction to the spermicide or lubricant, and in a few it's actually a latex allergy.

> Talk about nightmare firsts . . . I was one of many freshmen determined to make their long distance relationships work, so I was thrilled when my boyfriend came up to school for a visit. So thrilled, in fact, that I decided to make love with him. He had brought some condoms with him. So we were all set, right? Well, not quite. Neither of us had much experience with putting a condom on and in the passion of the moment, we were not about to read the instructions. He quickly put it on and then we were on our way. When we were removing the condom, we noticed a tear. I immediately froze with terror. How could something as wonderful as what we had just shared have such a terrible ending? We didn't know what to do. It was the middle of my cycle—prime time for pregnancy. I confided in a friend who told me about "the morning-after pill."

Within hours, I was at health services talking with a nurse about how the pill works and what the side effects are. I took the pill without hesitation, and it wasn't until later that night that I began to think about all the nurse had said. The pill, probably in addition to my nervousness over the situation, gave me horrible cramps and made me nauseous. This is one college experience I wish I'd never had. I try not to think about it anymore.

—Senior, Yale University

Diaphragm (with spermicide)—82–90 percent effective
What it is: A rubber dome, available by prescription only, that you insert into your vagina up to two hours before having sex. The diaphragm, which fully covers your cervix, must be used together with a spermicide.

Pros: There are no side effects, unless you are allergic to the latex or spermicide. Since the diaphragm can be inserted a couple of hours before sex, there's no need to interrupt when things get hot and heavy, if you've planned ahead.

Cons: Diaphragms are available by prescription only; you have to get fitted for one by your doctor. Diaphragms must be used with spermicide, and you have to reapply the spermicide before every time you have sex. They have a relatively high failure rate, partly because a lot of women have trouble getting the suckers up there. Inserting the diaphragm incorrectly lowers its effectiveness. It'll take time and practice before you perfect your technique. Finally, diaphragms do not provide adequate protection against STDs. If you want to play it safe, you'll need to use a condom as well.

Cervical Cap—82–90 percent effective
What it is: A latex dome that covers your cervix, like the diaphragm, but is made of thicker rubber and fits more closely.

Pros: Same as with a diaphragm, but cervical caps are sturdier. They can be left in place for 48 hours, and you don't need to apply more spermicide every subsequent time you have sex.

Cons: As with the diaphragm, you have to be fitted for a cervical cap by your doctor. Caps can be difficult to insert or remove, and don't protect you against STD transmission.

Other methods include spermicidal foams, creams, and jellies, but these are best used in conjunction with barrier contraceptive methods. When used with a condom or diaphragm, they can provide effective protection against the transmission of some STDs, including AIDS.

IF YOU THINK YOU'RE PREGNANT

No method of birth control is completely foolproof, and no matter how diligent you and your partner may be, it's always possible that one of the little suckers finds its way in. Early warning signs of pregnancy, besides a missed period, include fatigue, cramps, water retention, nausea or vomiting, and frequent urination.

Since some of these symptoms sound a hell of a lot like PMS, it may be hard to tell what's happening in your body. If your period is considerably late and you've (cringe) engaged in unprotected sex, the condom broke during sex, or you have some other reason to suspect you're pregnant, hightail it to a drugstore for a home pregnancy test or your college's health services for a confidential clinical test. If you are pregnant, the sooner you find out, the sooner you can discuss the matter with a doctor, and the more options you have.

If you do discover that you're pregnant, you face a range of choices, all of them difficult. Talk over your options with a doctor at your campus' infirmary. If you want more information, check the yellow pages for a Planned Parenthood in your area. You could also look for listings under "abortion services," "adoption agencies," or "family planning."

SEXUALLY TRANSMITTED DISEASES

The only 100 percent effective way to keep from contracting STDs is abstinence. If you do decide to have sex, the most effective way to prevent most STDs is by using a condom with spermicide containing Nonoxynol-9. If you think you may have an STD, or even if you just want more information, don't hesitate to stop by your campus' health services to get tested or talk to a doctor.

One of the greatest things about the health services at UConn is the women's clinic. Not only is it a full-fledged gynecological facility, offering most of the services found in ob/gyn offices, but the staff, comprised mainly of nurse practitioners and one or two part-time gynecologists, recognizes the sensitivities of our age group and the problems we face. Services like pelvic exams, blood tests, and various means of birth control, including the pill, dental dams, and condoms, are cheaper when bought through the infirmary; you also know that your situation will remain confidential, and that's a relief to those of us who feel we can't talk to our parents about these issues. The nurse practitioners are counselors, too: They can help educate students about issues like safe sex, birth control, and living with an STD.

—Senior, University of Connecticut

Here are some of the more common STDs:

Chlamydia

This bacterial infection is currently the most common curable STD nationwide. Chlamydia can occur simultaneously with gonorrhea, and its symptoms are similar: painful urination, discharge, or abdominal pain. Symptoms can be mild and disappear temporarily, only to recur later. Many infected women show no symptoms at all. An antibiotic usually clears up the infection, which can result in infertility if untreated.

Crabs (pubic lice)

Little bugs, each about 1/16 of an inch long, that attach themselves to pubic hair. Crabs can be transmitted sexually, or by jumping onto to you from infected sheets, towels, or clothes, and cause severe itching. You can get rid of your new friends by using a medicated soap or shampoo.

Genital warts

These highly contagious warts are caused by human papillova virus (HPV). They appear on or around the genitals or in the mouth (if transmitted through oral sex), and are spread through intimate body contact. Even if you or your partner is wearing a condom, you can contract genital warts, since they can appear in areas not covered by a condom. Genital warts may be visible and usually cause irritation and itching, but might cause no symptoms at all, especially in women. There is no cure; while warts can be removed chemically or surgically, they can grow back.

Gonorrhea

This bacterial infection spreads through contact with infected mucous membrane in the genitals, mouth, or throat. Symptoms may include painful urination and discharge, but there are often no symptoms at all, especially in women. A simple antibiotic will get rid of the infection, but if it goes untreated, it can result in major complications, ranging from infertility to blindness.

Hepatitis B

This viral infection is spread through contact with infected body fluids (including blood) and mucous membrane. An infected person might be asymptomatic at first, but eventually liver damage and even death can occur. The good news is, you can get vaccinated against hepatitis B. If you haven't had your hepatitis vaccination yet, your campus infirmary may offer the series of three shots at a reduced price.

Herpes

Both herpes I, which produces sores around the mouth, and herpes II, which produces sores in the genital area, are viral infections contracted through contact with an active sore or virus-carrying secretion. In addition to the sores, the virus can cause flulike symptoms including fevers, swollen glands, and muscle aches or pain. The virus is chronic; it can remain latent for months and then suddenly erupt into an outbreak. There is no cure, but there are drugs that help prevent recurrences.

Syphilis

Syphilis is a bacterial infection that can be transmitted through sexual contact or contact with infected blood, which means it can be passed through contaminated needles. The infection causes a canker sore on the genitals or mouth that is more detectable in men than in women, followed by flulike symptoms. Antiobiotics can cure syphilis, but if the disease is left untreated, it can cause serious complications, and even death.

HIV AND AIDS

People in our generation have been hearing about AIDS since we first learned where babies come from. The fact is, though, people our age are still contracting HIV (human immunodeficiency virus), the virus that causes AIDS, mostly through unprotected sex.

HIV is transmitted by certain types of sexual contact, including vaginal and anal sex. The risk of HIV transmission through oral sex is still uncertain, but seems small. You can also contract HIV by blood contact, through sharing needles for intravenous drug use, or through blood transfusions (the screening process has virtually eliminated this risks nowadays). You *can't* "catch AIDS" the way you catch a cold; there's no risk in casual contact with an infected person, and it's not airborne. HIV is a very fragile virus; it doesn't last long outside of the body. You can reduce your risk of contracting the virus by practicing safer sex by using latex condoms, and "dental dams" for oral sex on a woman, and always using sterile needles.

Early symptoms of HIV infection include flulike symptoms; a diagnosis of AIDS is made when the infected person's T cells, which defend against viruses, drop below a certain level, or he develops certain major complications. If you've engaged in any risky behaviors, you should definitely get tested as soon as possible. You can go to your campus' infirmary for a referral or a test, which detects antibodies to HIV in the blood. But keep in mind that getting a negative test result is no substitute for practicing safer sex.

Sex is omnipresent on college campuses; it finds its way into everything we do. The dating and sexual freedom of college life is one of its most unique (and anticipated) features for freshmen. College students tend to expand more than their intellectual horizons, and this is, within limits, totally healthy and normal. If you do choose to have sex, always keep yourself safe, through communication with your partner, and through smart decisions about sexual practices.

Health and Nutrition

To say that college is a hostile environment to a healthy lifestyle is an understatement. Freshmen who ate their vegetables every day and faithfully attended every track meet in high school one day wake up to notice a pooch that looks suspiciously like a beer belly. The caffeine flood and sleep deprivation that accompany an all-nighter wreak havoc on your system. And the close living quarters in the dorms means that germs spread from room to room faster than you can say "mono." This chapter covers the basics of keeping your body from succumbing to the attacks leveled on it every day by college life, from the notorious "Freshman 15" to the always poorly timed stomach flu.

Food, Nutrition, and Exercise

The "Freshman 15." You think it could never happen to you. But the grim reality is this: College can indeed expand more than your mind, and the combined effects of an increased intake of junk food and copious amounts of beer are often not pretty.

Just because, generally speaking, the food's bad in college doesn't mean you won't eat it. In fact, you'll probably eat a lot of it. And when you don't fill up on dining hall food, you might overcompensate later with pizza, cookies, or a bag of potato chips from the 24-hour convenience store that resides on every campus. To top it all off, more and more schools are encouraging fast food chains and cash operations like Taco Bell and Pizza Hut to set up shop on campus, meaning easy, late-night access to cheap but tasty grease.

The number of calories in your favorite fast food indulgences can approach four digits. Consume at your own risk:

- Burger King Chicken Sandwich: 685 calories
- Burger King Double Whopper with cheese: 935 calories
- Domino's Pizza (2 slices pepperoni): 447 calories
- McDonald's Big Mac: 500 calories
- McDonald's small french fries: 220 calories
- Taco Bell Taco Salad: 905 calories

—Source: U.S. Department of Agriculture

Let's face it, when you're juggling five classes, a job, relationships, and activities, pondering the food pyramid or the fiber content of your diet is probably not terribly high on your list of priorities. And at 2 A.M., with five pages of a seven-page paper left to go, a "Light" Taco Salad from Taco Bell with a large mocha to wash it down can seem pretty appealing. But too much of the wrong kinds of food at the wrong times can leave you lethargic and feeling unhappy with yourself. Here are some tips to help you survive the perils of college dining:

- Have breakfast. You might think you value sleep more than food, but getting up an extra fifteen minutes earlier so you can grab a bagel, a glass of juice, or a bowl of cereal can make you more alert and energetic for your morning classes.

- When faced with leftover chicken teriyaki or tuna surprise in the dining hall, be creative. Not eating at meals will only leave you craving junk food later. Make a huge salad, eat cereal (yes, for dinner), or go to the sandwich bar. Anything's better than leaving the dining hall hungry.

- Swipe portable, nutritious snacks from the dining hall (just make sure no one sees you). Bagels, little yogurt containers, and pieces of fruit make great snacks later on. Remember to bring your backpack to the table; hiding a banana under your shirt tends to raise suspicion.

- Make sensible substitutions. Replace high-fat, empty-calorie toppings or snacks with healthier versions. Top your baked potato with yogurt instead of sour cream, eat frozen yogurt instead of ice cream, put reduced-fat dressings on your salads. These small substitutions can make a big difference in your empty-calorie intake and add nutrients to your diet.

- Watch your caffeine and alcohol intake.
- Drink lots and lots of water.

Exercise

Collectively, college students tend to be an exercise-conscious group, but it's easy to let workouts go by the wayside when life gets busy. Even if you don't spend your afternoons sweatin' to the oldies, you can find plenty of active things to do on your campus. Here are some tips to help you burn something other than a hole in your couch:

- Play intramurals. Most campuses offer everything from coed football to inner-tube water polo to squash. Find something you like to do and go whenever you can, even if it's not on a regular basis.

- Drag a friend or roommate to the gym with you. You'll be less likely to bag on workouts if you've made plans to lift weights or take a dance class with a friend.

- Put a little more effort into daily activities. Take the stairs instead of taking the elevator. Walk to class instead of taking the shuttle. Jog for 20 minutes around the block. Hook up strenuously with your significant other. Every little bit helps.

Sleep

It seems that whenever a midterm, an extracurricular activity, or a hysterical long-distance love calls, sleep is the first thing to go out the window. Unfortunately, when you stay up for more than 24 hours, you become fatigued, your attention wanders, your concentration wanes, and you become less able to perform simple tasks, much less conjugate verbs in French. If you stay up for more than 60 hours in a row, you may experience headaches, blurred vision, or mood swings. So don't do it. Unless it's part of a university-sanctioned psychology experiment for which you'll be handsomely compensated.

A good night's sleep varies from person to person and averages about 7.5 hours. Get too much or too little sleep and you'll feel irritable and groggy, so you'll have to experiment to find out how much sleep leaves you feeling refreshed and alert. To keep from dozing in your ten-person seminar, keep the following in mind:

- Don't exercise less than a couple of hours before going to bed; exerting yourself can actually keep you awake rather than put you to sleep. Exercise in the morning may help you sleep better at night, though.

- Don't drink coffee or other caffeinated beverages before going to bed.

- If you've been drinking (and haven't passed out), wait until you sober up before you go to bed. Alcohol disturbs the sleep stages, and while you may go out like a light, you'll wake up the next morning feeling tired and hung over.

- Take naps. Even if you haven't taken a nap since kindergarten, you might want to consider getting back into the habit in college, when you're going to bed later than you did in high school, but have more free time in the afternoons. Limit your catnaps to an hour or so; sleeping more than that won't up the benefits and may actually leave you feeling more groggy, especially if it's an afternoon nap. Try napping in the early to mid afternoon, if you're tired and have that time free. Taking a nap too late in the day can interfere with that night's sleep.

Unfortunately, the reality of college life is that you'll occasionally be sleep deprived. On the plus side, even after long periods of staying awake, your body will recover with just one good night of sleep. Don't make all-nighters a habit, though; it can throw your internal clock off and leave you feeling tired and irritable.

IF YOU GET SICK

The bad news is, you will get sick in college. The worse news is, your mother won't be there to take care of you. And the worst news is, there is no good news. Getting sick at school just plain bites, and the only thing you can do is make sure you lessen the impact of whatever pestilence comes your way.

I came to Ithaca, NY from Minnesota, so I was certain that I could handle the weather. I did not feel it necessary to wear a hat or gloves in the comparatively tropical land of upstate New York. Heck, it was 15 degrees, far warmer than the minus 10 my hometown of Minneapolis was experiencing. I thought my bravery would gain me respect, but all it got me was a bad case of the flu.

Trying to handle a chemical engineering load and play a sport while your nose is running, your lungs are full of fluid, and your chest feels like an entire percussion section, is a near impossibility. I ended up bedridden for nearly a week due to my stupid disregard for Mother Nature. I had to push off my midterms, skip two weeks of practice, and, even worse, lose my reputation as the cold-weather tough guy. The flu seems like such an innocuous little sickness, but when it hits, it hits hard, and when you fall to it, you fall hard. Sure, it doesn't have the ring of mono or even strep throat, but you still have to go through all of the pain.

—Senior, Cornell University

YOUR HEALTH PLAN

As a student, you'll probably receive automatic primary care services at your campus' health facility, and be required to purchase either a supplemental hospitalization plan from the health center, or show that you have an alternate insurance plan (usually your parents' insurance will cover you as long as you remain a full-time student). Review your parents' plan and compare it to your school's supplemental coverage, which is probably $200 to $400 per semester. Your parents' insurance might not fully cover expensive services like allergy shots or physical therapy out-of-state.

Your campus' health center should provide a range of services, from 24-hour urgent care, to immunizations, to gynecological services, to nutrition counseling, to mental hygiene. There probably will be doctors or nurse practitioners available 24 hours a day, seven days a week to see you or refer you somewhere else, if necessary. Although walk-in care should always be available, you might not be seen immediately during busy times like flu season, so make an appointment as soon as you realize you're sick.

You might be reluctant to go to the doctor, especially for what seems like just a little cold. Often with common college maladies, a health practitioner can't do much anyway, except send you home with a box of Kleenex and a bottle of Tylenol. If you have any of the following symptoms, though, over-the-counter remedies are not going to cut it, and you should see a doctor as soon as possible.

- If you have a relatively high fever (at least 101 degrees)
- If you've been puking for more than 24 hours, and have not been able to keep down food or water
- If you have ear pain, especially if accompanied by fever or a sore throat
- If you have a persistent cough that has lasted more than a couple of days
- If you have severe or persistent muscle or joint pain that's not caused by too many minutes on the Stairmaster or by menstrual cramps
- If you have any symptoms of the sexually transmitted diseases (STDs) described in chapter 15, including painful urination, and bumps, warts, or sores on the genitalia

Some common maladies that afflict college students, along with their symptoms and remedies/treatments, are listed below.

The common cold
Ah, you know the symptoms far too well. Sneezing, runny nose, congestion, general tiredness. Unfortunately, there's not much you can do about this besides huddle up in bed with a box of tissues and and some over-the-counter antihistamines. Don't forget that antihistamines can make you drowsy, so don't operate any heavy machinery while you're taking them. And don't expect to get much reading done, either.

Influenza (the flu)
The flu is a contagious viral infection spread when an infected person (i.e., your roommate, boyfriend, or the freak that sits next to you in Latin) expels the virus into the air by sneezing or coughing, and you inhale the particles. Sounds pleasant, doesn't it? You can also get the flu

through direct hand contact with someone who's got it. Symptoms include fever, chills, weakness, loss of appetite, muscle aches, a dry throat, and nausea. The fever can often climb to 104 degrees but usually goes down after a few days. Bacterial complications of the flu, such as bacterial pneumonia or sinus and ear infections, can develop. Go to the doctor to get checked out, but if you have uncomplicated flu, she won't be able to do much for you besides recommend acetaminophen to reduce your fever and relieve your pain. You'll have to suffer until it runs its course. If you have a bacterial complication from the flu, your doctor can prescribe an antibiotic.

SHOULD YOU GET A FLU SHOT?

You can reduce your chances of getting laid up by the flu during midterms by getting a flu shot—a vaccine that contains the flu viruses that scientists expect to cause flu outbreaks that year. A flu shot is about 75 percent effective in preventing the flu, but if you are in the unlucky minority, the vaccine can make your symptoms less severe.

The best time to get a flu shot is mid-October to mid-November. Your campus' health clinic might publicize this service, which could even be free to students. Few people have complications to a flu vaccine, but you can develop a slight fever or headache that usually subsides in a couple of days.

Mononucleosis (mono)

They don't call it the kissing disease for nothing. Spread through saliva, infectious mono can be caused by several agents, although the Epstein-Barr Virus (EBV) causes 95 percent of adult cases. Early symptoms of mono include feeling generally rundown and loss of appetite. Later symptoms include mono's notorious unshakeable fatigue, sore throat, swollen glands, fever, and muscle aches. Complications like an enlarged spleen, strep throat, or inflammation of the liver or jaundice may also develop in some cases. If you have any of these symptoms, go see your doctor for a diagnosis; you'll get a preliminary blood test, and even if your first test comes out negative, you might have to take a later one if your symptoms persist. A significant percentage of adults with mono test negative the first time around. If you do have mono, your doctor will prescribe adequate rest and a pain reliever like acetaminophen. The duration of the illness varies from person to person; about one-third of college students who get mono don't have to stay in bed at all because their symptoms are so mild. Even if you do have to stay in the infirmary or in your own bed, you'll probably be up and around in a couple of weeks. Fatigue usually lasts for two to three months after you've gotten better, so it's important to get plenty of rest and eat well even after you've resumed normal activities.

> What's the single worst thing that can happen to you freshman year of college? That's right—mono. And I got it. Big time. Right before finals at the end of my freshman year, my throat started to hurt pretty badly. At first, I thought I just had a cold, so I went to student health. Sure enough, they told me I had mono. "No way," I thought. "This can't be happening to me." I tried to tell myself that student health was mistaken in its diagnosis—after all, you could walk into student health with a broken leg and they'd tell you that you had mono. Besides, I hadn't really participated in any of what everybody usually takes to be the "requisite activities" for mono infection. However, after I began to sleep an average of 20 hours a day, I began to realize that student health may indeed have been right. Miraculously, I pulled respectable grades on all of my finals. I say "miraculously" because the four hours a day that I actually managed to stay awake were, for the most part, monopolized by Sega Genesis—the only activity that I had enough energy for. Somehow, I made it home at the end of the term, and I slept for about two weeks straight.
>
> —Junior, Georgetown University

EATING DISORDERS

College students, particularly women, tend to be very vulnerable to eating disorders, the most common of which are anorexia nervosa (self-starvation) and bulimia (binging and purging). For students who suffer from these disorders, self-esteem becomes so closely tied to their weight and dieting success that they find themselves trapped in a dangerous cycle of repeated and compulsive food-related behavior.

Signs of eating disorders include an obsession with eating, food, weight, and body image. A person with an eating disorder might count and recount calories at every meal, step on the scale several times a day, and complain of feeling fat even when her weight is normal or extremely low. Students with eating disorders often engage in rigid or ritualistic behaviors related to food, and may feel anxious eating in front of other people—you may notice that a friend only nibbles at food at dinner, or has stopped going to the dining hall altogether. For many college students dealing with new stresses, managing food or weight becomes a matter of staying in control.

Symptoms and Effects of Eating Disorders

Anorexia

Anorectics, though often emaciated, are afraid to gain weight. They show symptoms associated with severe weight loss, including dry hair and skin, cold hands and feet, digestive problems, difficulty sleeping, and amenorrhea (cessation of menstruation). If an anorectic does not get help, more severe problems like stress fractures (from lack of calcium), ketosis (severe chemical imbalance), and a potentially fatal weakness of the heart muscle may develop.

Bulimia

Bulimics usually weigh about average or slightly above average, but have rapid weight gains and losses. The disorder is characterized by secret binging and purging through self-induced vomiting, abuse of laxatives or diuretics, fasting, or overexercising. These purging methods can cause a number of medical problems, including dehydration, constipation and digestive disorders, dental problems (from repeated vomiting), and muscle weakness.

If You Think You Have an Eating Disorder

Most college students go on diets once in a while and are conscious about their weight and appearance. If this consciousness escalates to the point of becoming a large part of your life, you might have a problem. Very few people can break the cycle of an eating disorder on their own; most need help. But it can be really hard, even if you recognize that your eating habits have gotten out of control, to seek help, and it's all too easy to feel you're alone on a college campus. If you think your eating habits are making you sick, anxious, or depressed, get some support, even if you just start by confiding in a friend. If your school doesn't have a confidential eating disorders hotline, there are nutritionists or counselors on every college campus, as well as support groups with other students who've dealt with similar problems. Probably the easiest way to get in touch with someone is by calling your school's health services clinic.

Helping a Friend

If you suspect a friend might have an eating disorder, the most important thing to do is to communicate. Talk to her informally about your concerns, and focus on health, rather that on food or weight. Let her know that she has your support, and that there is outside help available too. Definitely acknowledge the weight loss, though—ignoring it may make her think that her efforts are failing and cause her to try even harder. Before you confront your friend about your concerns, call your school's eating disorder hotline or talk to someone at health services about how to approach the situation.

Even if you confront your friend about your worries or concerns, she may deny that there's a problem. If you feel like the conversation's going the wrong way, try to end it before one of you gets angry at the other, and in such a way that you can bring the issue up again at a later point. If she resists acknowledging the problem to you, remind yourself that ultimately you can't be responsible for handling your friend's problem. Know your limits and know when to back off, and consider serious measures, like calling a roommate's parents, only if the situation has escalated to a serious level.

DEPRESSION

The prevalence of depression among college students is alarming. Being away from home for the first time, falling in love and dealing with breakups, and academic and financial pressures can cause bouts of low self-esteem and make you feel completely overwhelmed. In most cases, these feelings subside with time, but for some college students depression persists for weeks, and leads to self-destructive thoughts or behavior. Common causes of depression among college students include low self-esteem brought on by parents' divorce, the breakup of a relationship, the death of a friend or family member, and academic or financial stress.

Some symptoms of depression include feeling persistently sad, anxious, hopeless, and pessimistic; an academic slide; withdrawal from friends or a romantic relationship; trouble sleeping; loss of appetite or weight; chronic headaches and other physical symptoms that don't respond to treatment; and thoughts of suicide. Depressives also sometimes act out in self-destructive ways, such as abusing drugs or alcohol, or having unsafe sex.

If You Are Depressed

If you find yourself experiencing some of the feelings listed above, consider contacting a counselor or therapist through you school's health services. Everything you talk about will be kept confidential, so don't worry about personal information getting around. Often the hardest part of dealing with depression is taking the first step and doing something about it. Talking to a good friend or a therapist can help you understand what's bothering you, and get you headed towards feeling better.

Helping a Friend Who is Depressed or Suicidal

If you think your friend might be depressed, make him aware that you're willing to listen and provide support. Don't try to give advice or take charge of the situation; you can't become responsible for your friend's depression. But let him know that you're there to listen. Ask questions. Back off if you feel that either one of you is getting angry, but don't be afraid to tactfully follow up at some later point. If your friend does open up to you, don't be dismissive of his problems or overly cheerful, although you should reassure him that depression is treatable and temporary.

If you think your friend is *seriously* depressed or suicidal, you might want to talk to someone at your health service's mental health clinic about where to go from there. If you believe your friend is suicidal, get that person professional help immediately, by contacting your health clinic, a suicide hotline, or a hospital emergency room.

WARNING SIGNS OF A POTENTIAL SUICIDE ATTEMPT

- Displaying signs of serious depression
- Engaging in high-risk, self-destructive activities
- Giving away prized possessions
- Discussing suicide, or becoming preoccupied with death or the afterlife
- Obtaining the means for committing suicide, by purchasing a gun or stocking up on sleeping pills

The stresses and strains of college life can wreak havoc on both your mental and physical health. For college students, health tends to fall low on the list of priorities, after classes, friends, activities, jobs, and partying. It's not until you get sick that you realize how much illness can frustrate all of those aspects of your life. So take care of yourself, from the start.

Campus Safety

As the city crime beat reporter for my school's daily newspaper, I went pretty much anywhere the story was. I always tried to justify my pursuits in the name of good journalism. It didn't matter the place or the time—whether it was way off campus at 11:00 P.M. to investigate a rape, or through gang territory to interview prostitutes. Never did I feel endangered at all. But one day, my luck ran out.

I was actually on what I thought was one of my less risky ventures into a poor region of the city. I wasn't that far from campus, and it was a bright, sunny afternoon. A man no older than I am, with one leg of his sweat pants rolled up to his knee and a bright red towel draped over his head, approached me. He kindly informed me I shouldn't be walking around alone in the neighborhood. He told me he would be my friend and, catch this, protect me from getting shot—by him. And the only catch was, I had to give him all my money.

On a personal level, my mugging has made me more wary about walking through some city neighborhoods in the heady manner of my sophomore days. But the experience was also an interesting close to my education about city crime.

Walking alone on a dangerous street isn't the brightest thing to do, but staying within the walls of your university is dangerously limiting. There's a difference between being cautious and hiding.

—Senior, Yale University

Campus security. You sit dutifully through the mandatory security orientation as some cop enumerates the dos and donts of campus safety in a monotone flatter than you imagined possible. You get the information booklet at registration, and without so much as giving it a second glance, nonchalantly toss it into the nearest wastepaper basket or recycling bin. You nod attentively at your mother's parting warnings, tucking away the key chain–sized container of pepper spray she hands you as a final goodbye gift.

It's pretty easy to ignore the freshman year onslaught of warnings about campus security, and even easier to lose sight of common-sense precautions as you spend more time at school. That is, until you walk into your room one day and find it's somewhat emptier than when you left it. Or until you watch your roommate deal with the friendly folks at the bank after leaving her purse—and her credit cards—unattended for the briefest of moments.

Realistically, crime does happen on college campuses, both those in big cities and those in less urban environments. You can try to gauge the safety at your school by looking at its crime logs—the 1990 Student Right-to-Know and Campus Security Act requires all colleges and universities receiving federal financial aid to report crimes such as burglary, robbery, rape, and murder, as well as to release statements on security policies and procedures. But keep in mind it's hard to compare one school to another on the basis of crime statistics, and numbers often are not the best indicators of relative safety on college campuses. Rates and types of crime and official security measures depend a lot on whether a school is rural or urban, residential or commuter.

Wherever you are, there are conscious steps you can take to protect yourself and your stuff. This chapter is not meant to generate paranoia; most college campuses are relatively safe. But there are definitely common-sense measures you should take to avoid harm to your person or property, both in the dorms, and when you hit the streets surrounding your college.

The one overriding thing you should remember, whether you're in your room, in your car, or walking or jogging on the street: Stay alert, and follow your instincts. Nothing can substitute for common sense.

IN THE DORMS

Lock your doors.

Your dorm room. Your pad. Your study space. Your love den. Chances are you'll spend more time in your dorm room than anywhere else. It will become your cozy haven where you feel warm and fuzzy and safe. And more often than not, you'll feel comfortable leaving the door to your room unlocked or the gate to your building propped open.

Bad move.

In most crimes that actually take place in dormitories, both thefts and personal attacks, someone who lived in the building left more than the proverbial door open.

As inviting as it is to leave your door open while you run down the hall to shower, if you want to own more than your towel when you get back, resist temptation. Leaving your door open poses a number of risks, and is a bad idea on any campus.

Don't let strangers into into your building.

At the beginning of this year, an unemployed resident of New Haven offered to help me unload my minivan at the beginning of the school year. He introduced himself and explained that he was currently out of work and would move my belongings for a couple of slices from a nearby pizzeria. After considering how I might be able to carry all my stuff, including a couch and refrigerator all the way up to the top floor by myself, I accepted his offer. For the next 20 minutes, he and I lugged all my junk up three flights of stairs, only pausing long enough to wipe the sweat from our hands. When we were done, I handed him the $10 I had on me him and apologized, saying I was hoping to give him twice as much.

But that's not the last I heard from him. Later that same night, he was heard outside of the gate calling my name and asking people where I was. Over the next week, I received phone calls from him asking for the other $10 that I wanted to give him. He had returned to my room and left messages on my door. I was a little disturbed to discover that he had been in my dorm and that he knew how to reach me by phone and in person. Not only did he know where I live and the contents of my room, he knew my name and could use that as a means of getting into my entryway.

The next time he called, I met him outside with the rest of the money. A week later, he called again and asked for a few dollars to pay for bus fare. I told him that I couldn't afford to give him any more money and didn't expect to hear from him any more. And so far, I haven't.

While nothing bad actually resulted from my interaction with this stranger, there was definitely potential for unpleasant situations. I tell this story only as an example of how one must become aware of the environment in which one lives. What might be safe in one city or in one circumstance might not be in another. While I will continue to greet passersby and respond to the requests of the homeless with civil answers, I am more conscious of the limitations that should be imposed on these exchanges.

—Senior, Yale University

Some urban schools, like Columbia University and the University of Pennsylvania, hire security guards to check identification cards at building entrances, and require students to sign in all guests. But at most colleges, keeping freak shows out of the dormitories is the responsibility of the students who live there.

If you see someone who you don't think belongs, ask questions. It may seem rude, and you may be embarrassed when the person turns out to be your hallmate's boyfriend, but better safe than sorry.

Along the same lines, don't hesitate to ask someone trying to gain access into your dorm his reason for being there, whom he's visiting, or even to show student identification before letting them in the door. Not doing so not only compromises your safety, but also the safety of the people you live with.

Be careful in isolated areas such as elevators, stairwells, or basements.
The most important thing to remember here is to follow your instincts. If at any point you feel uneasy when you are alone with someone in an elevator or on a stairwell, get off at the next floor. Many dormitory basements have laundry facilities, student lounges, or vending machines. If you are ever alone in one of these areas, particularly if you are a woman, be aware of your surroundings and be ready for a hasty exit of you ever feel threatened.

In 1995, two Yale University juniors were robbed at gunpoint as they watched cartoons in their residence hall's basement TV lounge during the hectic fall semester moving-in period. Someone had propped the gate to get into the courtyard, the door at the entrance to the building, and the door leading into the basement.

Engrave or register valuables with your university's police department.
Many universities encourage students to register expensive items such as computers and bicycles with them, and will engrave your social security number on such items in case they are stolen and later recovered.

ON THE STREETS

> I think New York City is safer than rural Geneseo to walk around. No matter how many crazy people there are around, at least there are people.
>
> —Senior, New York University

Don't walk alone at night.
Always, always walk with someone else at night, particularly if you are a woman. Drag your roommate out for coffee with you. Coerce your friend into walking you home from a party. Make it a habit. You can also always take advantage of the late-night campus escort programs or shuttle services many schools offer.

Avoid running alone, especially through unlit or isolated areas like woods or empty parks.
Many colleges have running clubs, and even if yours doesn't, it's pretty easy to find a jogging partner or even to coordinate groups of runners.

When walking or running alone, be alert and follow your instincts.
OK. You've violated rules number 1 and number 2. When you're walking alone, particularly at night, walk confidently and purposefully. Avoid shortcuts through questionable, isolated, or poorly lit areas. Constantly be aware of your surroundings, and if you feel uneasy, follow your instincts. Head for populated areas, or look for campus phones with one-touch direct access to the police. At most schools, these emergency phones, often distinguished by a blue light, are located at half-block intervals.

Schools in rural or suburban communities are not necessarily safer than those in urban environments. In fact, it's even more crucial to be cautious and alert in less populated areas.

> It's a big campus and people often go cross-country running where there are few buildings. I've seen people running through the woods at 1:30, 2:30 in the morning, and they think it's safe until something happens. Don't be so trusting.
>
> —Senior, Stanford University

Try not to wear very expensive jewelry on the street, and keep valuables like notebook computers concealed.
Sure, those handy powerbook carrying cases are convenient, but they practically scream "Steal me!" If you're walking through a sketchy part of town, stow the computer in your backpack, or leave it at home. And wearing valuables expensive jewelry on the street makes you a target for obvious reasons.

Be careful at the cash machine.
For college students, ATM cards become more valuable than blood, and as integral a part of college life as dirty laundry and procrastination. You will use the ATM. Frequently. Particularly if your parents feed the account. But keep in mind that people at cash machines are easy targets, because they are distracted, and, well, because they have cash.

Be aware of what's going on around you before, during, and after your transaction, and don't make the transaction if the machine is in an isolated location or if anyone is behaving suspiciously near you. After you've emptied your account, put your money, card, and receipt away immediately, before leaving the machine.

And don't forget to take your card out of the machine when you're done. (Yes, it happens. We've lived it.)

Keep a close eye on your belongings.
Remember to watch your belongings in public places like restaurants or libraries. Bookbags, purses, and notebook computers are especially popular items.

Lock your bike.
Bike theft is a common crime on campus, especially urban campuses. You can secure your bike by buying an insured U-lock, attaching it to university-sanctioned bike racks, or leaving it only in well-lighted, heavily foot-trafficked areas.

Protect your (other) wheels.
Park your car in well-lighted, heavily foot-trafficked areas. Make sure no valuables are visible from the outside of the car, and obviously, make sure the windows are rolled up and doors locked when you park.

If it Happens . . .

If you are the victim of theft, report it to the police and campus dean's office right away, particularly if your keys were stolen. Many colleges have electronic access cards instead of conventional keys, and if your card is stolen, you can have it deactivated immediately.

Remember to cancel any credit cards and inform your bank if you are missing your checkbook.

If you are the victim of a violent crime, again, contact the police immediately. They will find you medical attention if necessary, and help you contact friends or family members.

SEXUAL ASSAULT

FBI CRIME STATISTICS

- Seventy-five percent of campus rapes were committed by someone the victim knew.
- Fifty-seven percent of rapes of college-age women occur on dates.
- Ninety percent of campus sexual assaults involved alcohol or drugs.

In the overwhelming majority of rape cases on college campus, the perpetrator is someone the woman knows, and in many cases, the rape takes place on a date. But a rape can be committed by a stranger, an acquaintance, a friend, or a lover—if sex happens against your will, without consent, or with forced consent, it is rape, and it is punishable by law. Rape is never the victim's fault, but there are steps you can take to protect yourself against this kind of assault, particularly if you are on a date or with someone you know.

- Trust your instincts. As soon as a situation begins to feel uncomfortable, threatening, or wrong, get out of it.
- Take your own car on dates if you can.
- Let your roommate or another friend know where you're going, who you're going with, and when you expect to be back.
- Communicate your limits clearly and assertively.
- Avoid drinking or doing drugs excessively; it impairs your ability to communicate and think clearly enough to get yourself out of a threatening situation.

If you are raped, as difficult as it might be, it's imperative that you seek medical help. Find a friend to confide in and accompany you to your school's health services clinic. Don't bathe, shower, or change your clothes before you go. The doctors there will examine you for external and internal injuries, test you for pregnancy and STDs, gather medical evidence if you decide you want to press charges, and offer counseling services.

The weeks after a rape are filled with emotional trauma; seeing a counselor or just talking out your feelings with a friend can help. There are rape crisis hotlines you can call to talk to someone anonymously and confidentially, and most campuses have support groups in addition to regular counseling services. It's crucial to recognize that it wasn't your fault. No one deserves to be raped.

STAYING SAFE

Not all crimes are avoidable, but there are definite measures you can take to keep yourself safe. Be aware of your surroundings, to trust your instincts, and avoid taking unnecessary risks. Happily, most college students make it through all four (or five, or six) years without incident. With any luck, the closest you'll come to being a crime victim will be when your roommate raids your closet without your permission.

THE MINORITY EXPERIENCE

So you've bubbled in the circle on your application that most closely matches your ethnicity; now what? Well, there is no way to say exactly what the minority experience is at every school. To describe the college life of the thousands of Asian, Latino, African American and Native American students would be as daunting a task as describing each individual snowflake. But just as you can say that snow is cold, you can say that there are some common opportunities, resources, and problems that many minority students encounter when they get to campus.

Don't be fooled by the term *minority*. Usually it refers to groups traditionally underrepresented at the college level. But even at schools where your ethnic group may be only five percent of the student body, the actual number of students who share your background could reach into the hundreds. Although it can be very unnerving to enroll in a school where students who share your background compose only five or eight percent of the student body, you might be pleasantly surprised at the actual numbers of students on hand at freshmen preenrollment programs that bubbled in the same circle you did. For students who hail from high schools where they were the one representative of their ethnic group, a larger community can be comforting.

At first I was a little intimidated by the enormity of the campus and the number of students who were not minorities. But since I came from a private school in Manhattan where I was one of two Asian students, I settled in pretty quickly. It's different being a minority at college, because even though the percentages are low, the number of students is actually quite large. Now, I'm one of hundreds.

—Senior, Yale University

Visiting schools will give you a feel for the size of the community you will be joining. Be careful not to base all your judgments about a school on the view book mailed to you with your application. Despite pictures of many minority students in university brochures, the scene can be a different one when you arrive on campus.

THE SUPPORT NETWORK

Most campuses have deans of minority affairs who will be available to offer advice, hear concerns, and help you deal with the transition to college life. Although they can help you handle any of the challenges you'll face at college, they usually focus on issues unique to helping students of color adjust to campus. An added bonus is that deans of minority affairs might share your race or ethnicity, whereas other administrators may not. Take advantage of the experience and advice these people have to offer, especially if you feel more comfortable dealing with counselors who share a common heritage with you.

Most schools also have formalized mentoring programs for incoming freshmen. In August, your school might assign seniors or juniors to freshmen of the same or similar background. These ethnic or minority affairs counselors can help you settle into the campus and start to find your niche. Usually, these peer advisors are assigned in addition to the freshman counselors or R.A.'s assigned to all incoming students. Many schools hope ethnic counselors will ease the culture shock for students who hail from homogeneous high schools, or just provide a comforting, familiar face for students accustomed to being the singular representative of their race in academic settings. Of course, if no specific minority advisor has been assigned to you, feel free to seek out minority freshmen counselors or bring your questions to upperclassmen in your courses.

Also, some schools with cultural centers or ethic student unions will hold study breaks for minority students to meet each other and discuss cultural issues of relevance to the community. Talking to upperclassmen in these social settings is a good way to figure out the political strength of your community on campus.

SPECIAL HOUSING OPTIONS

Chances are, you'll be housed with a mix of people from different backgrounds. The blend may cause some culture shock at first, but after the beginning weeks you should get used to each other's idiosyncrasies. Whether you speak to your parents in Spanish on the phone or your parents leave messages in Korean on the answering machine, the diversity of your dorm will offer a great deal of cultural exposure for you and the people you encounter. You might even find yourself picking up your Southern roommates' phrase "fixin' to go to dinner" or teaching your suitemate mah-jongg (a Chinese game of tiles).

Some schools allow you to take a little of the guess work out of your housing plan. The University of Pennsylvania, for example, allows students to live in same-race housing at its W. E. B. Du Bois dorm, which predominantly houses African American students, while other houses contain predominantly Asian or Latino students who choose this option. Other schools mail out rooming preference forms on which you can indicate before you matriculate your interest in having a roommate of the same race or culture.

> Living with a Chinese roommate was more of an emotional decision. I thought it would be nice to have a Chinese roommate so that we could share the newspaper and have common food tastes. She would understand that Chinese food was not at all about fried rice or general tso chicken.
>
> —Senior, Yale University

While you will miss out on the diversity and cultural exposure you'd get with randomly assigned housing in the dorms, same-race housing is a choice you should seriously consider if you would like a cultural partner with whom to face the early days of college life. Another route to same-race housing is through ethnic fraternities and sororities. At some schools where the ethnic fraternities do not have a house proper, the brothers and sisters move into off-campus apartments together.

ETHNIC OR CULTURAL ACTIVITIES

Your dorm room isn't the only place you can find venues to chat about and bond over cultural similarities or a common upbringing. Early on you can look into the possibility of joining or forming cultural and ethnic groups, writing for literary magazines, or acting in performance troupes for people of color. Through these activities with a focus on culture and race, you'll meet classmates with similar interests in your heritage and community involvement. Participation in ethnic associations will usually entail attending weekly meetings, planning annual events or forums, and pinpointing problem areas on campus for members of your ethnic group. Many organizations will sponsor speakers' series, fashion shows, parties, and career advising. On any one campus you might be able to choose from the Black Undergraduate Law Society, National Society for Black Engineers, or the Premedical Society for Latinos, among others. Getting involved with these groups will also allow you to meet people in small groups, an invaluable opportunity in an large campus environment.

> The writers and editors on my literary magazine for women of color have become fast friends. I have lunch dates, movie partners, roommates and life-long friends rolled into one.
>
> —Sophomore, Northeastern University

Through ethnic fraternities and sororities, some students even find new, extended siblings. The role of black or Latino greek life varies from campus to campus, but in most places they sponsor campus-wide parties and perform in regular "step shows," where the brothers or sisters create different rhythms and beats using hand clapping and feet stomping. The shows are very popular in the African American and Latino communities in particular, and tend to draw large numbers at each performance, making them a great way to meet people. Cultural fraternities can also provide you with membership to powerful national organizations and a worldwide network of minority college graduates.

Even if you aren't looking for permanent membership, but still wish to belong to a national organization with an intercollegiate flavor, there are other alternatives. Annual Asian pride conferences at different campuses attract participants from nearby universities, while more high-profile groups like the American Civil Liberties Union can get students from all 50 states attending its annual events. If you join the debate association and compete on the collegiate circuit, you'll find yourself bonding with minority debaters from other schools. Thanks to newsgroups on the Internet and E-mail, membership in national groups is far more feasible than in the past. Conferences can be planned, friendships cultivated, and information disseminated without incurring the cost of stamps or long-distance telephone calls. If you would like to see some new group of minority students get together—say, a national conference of minority student journalists—with a little planning and funding from minority groups and cultural deans, you can make that event happen. You should also look to university-wide administrators for funding and campus space to hold events. Many schools are willing and enthusiastic to have their school host national conferences or help you create a new organization.

Of course, there is no one track to getting involved in your community on campus or exploring your identity. Many minority students forgo the cultural groups in favor of more mainstream campus activities like the daily paper or debate associations.

> Sometimes you need to do your own thing. Join a group and make your statement that way. I teach dance to inner-city kids in Boston and also tutor at a local public school. Being with those kids has really allowed me to put into perspective what it means to be a Latina at Harvard, and I've been able to show the kids that they can make it too.
>
> —Senior, Harvard University

The flip side of choosing not to join groups like the African Pride Union or Despierta Boriqua, a political action group for Puerto Rican students, is that you may face criticism from others involved in those groups that you aren't doing enough for your community. Despite this pressure, it's important to be your own person, and feel comfortable making choices that are right for you. If you want to side-step the world of step shows and instead walk onto center stage to act in campus-wide plays or rush singing groups—just do it. You'll be infinitely more happy doing things that you enjoy rather than trying to gain the approval of a particular group of people. If you join an activity that you truly enjoy you'll also tend to contribute much more to the organization. For the most part, you'll find support from your friends and classmates in whatever area in which you choose to excel.

ACADEMIC OPPORTUNITIES

College life affords opportunities outside the dorm room or the cultural house to explore your interests in your heritage and culture. Many schools support ethnic studies programs like African American or Latin American studies and allow students to declare majors in these areas. With the campaign for added ethnic studies courses and majors spreading across the country, the availability of this type of specific study will likely increase in coming years. If you choose to earn a diploma in ethnic studies you may find yourself learning Hindi or studying Mambo in a classroom setting with leading experts in the field. This type of study will also give you the opportunity to get to know minority faculty members and gain insight not only into what it means to be a member of that particular ethnic group, but also what it means to be a member of that particular ethnic group on your college campus. Minority faculty can serve as a fountain of information on available scholarships or fellowships for travel to, say, Africa or Latin America during the summer or spring break—for research, of course. They may also be able to write recommendation letters for summer programs or for graduate and professional schools in your senior year.

Many traditional majors like English and History now require courses in Latin American literature or Native American history, so that even if you didn't major in an ethnic study, you won't miss the opportunity to integrate your culture into your academic life. You might also look into the possibility of independent study projects, if there is an area or issue that you would like to explore, but can't find a course that fits your interest. For minority students whose ethnicity includes a bilingual tradition, language courses can be a wonderful way to brush up on your written Japanese or your spoken Spanish. One woman we know who spoke Chinese at home, but never learned to write it, took Chinese for two years without telling her parents. Then, on Mother's Day she penned a letter to her mother in Chinese as a gift. On the other hand, if you're fluent in your native tongue, language courses can also provide high grades with which to pad a lagging G.P.A.

ACADEMIC STRESS

The classroom can also be a source of stress for minority students, who may find themselves lone representatives of their ethnic group in a seminar or class section of 25 to 30 students.

> You don't feel the racial difference until you are sitting in classes when slavery or O. J. Simpson comes up. Most of my teachers are white and there aren't many black students in my class, so eyes turn to you and you have to represent.
>
> —Senior, Temple University

Prepare ahead of time to handle this sort of discomfort and tension in a way that suits you. Feel no pressure to speak on behalf of the entire African American race or play the role of Mexican Americans everywhere. If you have a viewpoint, express it; if you don't, say, "Hey, why is everyone looking at me?" In any case, you should never feel unable to take a class because there aren't enough minority students in it. Lecture courses generally will not focus much attention on the individual, so being the only minority in a large class shouldn't be much of an issue. Of course, if you remember to be yourself, and keep a sense of humor, being the only minority shouldn't be much of a problem, even in smaller classes. In fact, the experience may help you cement who you are outside of your ethnic community or gain insight into how your cultural background has shaped your views.

In almost every experience or obstacle you face as a minority on campus, remember that if you are having cash flow problems because you have to send money home to your parents, or need to figure out how to get a group started on your campus, there is someone there who faced the same challenges and figured out a solution. You are not alone. A minority dean may be able to help you deal more effectively with the financial aid office, an upperclassmen may be able to point you in the right direction of a more sympathetic administrator to whom you should pitch your ideas. Being a minority at college comes with a built-in support network that other students don't have, perhaps because these ethnic communities are smaller. At the Massachusetts Institute of Technology, where Latino students are five percent of the population and black students only two percent, one senior said the communities are "a very close-knit family."

If you've chosen not to attend one of the many same-race or same-gender colleges, take advantage of the diversity of your campus. You may very well have the benefit of both worlds as a student at a mixed campus: you'll enjoy a sense of community, and you'll also have the opportunity to challenge some of your assumptions by meeting and befriending classmates of different races.

GAY AND LESBIAN STUDENTS

If you're a gay man, a lesbian, or a bisexual student, you'll also be part of a minority group on campus, and face some of the same problems that members of ethnic and racial minorities face. Campuses vary tremendously in their acceptance of gay and lesbian students; it's important to get a feel for the political tilt of a campus before you matriculate. Generally, politically liberal schools in the Northeast tend to be more accepting of students who are openly gay, although that's obviously an enormous generalization with plenty of exceptions.

Although chances are you won't get the benefits of the officially sanctioned support network often available to ethnic and racial minority students, at most schools there is a support network out there for you. Many campuses have very active groups of gay, lesbian, and bisexual students, which may sponsor outside speakers, forums, and social functions. Other organizations may just offer a place for students to come and talk. If you are having trouble coming to terms with your sexual orientation, or if you're concerned about coming out to family and friends, there are very likely anonymous student-run hotlines you can call to discuss your feelings. You might also want to seek out a trusted friend, or an openly gay upperclassman who's been in the same position you're in now, to gain some perspective.

Coming out is an extremely personal decision, but many gay students find it an enormous relief to come out to their roommates and friends at school, and, if they haven't already, to family and friends at home. Generally speaking, you'll probably be better off telling your roommates sooner than later. There are no guarantees as to their reactions, but chances are your roommates will be far more supportive and accepting than you expect. If you're having a lot trouble telling your roommate, you might be better off waiting until an appropriate moment—say, when she suggests setting you up with a blind date.

Your sexual orientation is a big part of your identity, and will therefore shape your college experience. The important thing is to take control of the way in which it shapes that experience; to make it, if it isn't already, something you're comfortable with. Finding other students who share some of your feelings and experiences can help you make the most of your four years at school, as well as the years beyond college.

STUDENTS WITH DISABILITIES

If you're a student with a disability, you're not alone: Nearly nine percent of the 1994 freshman class described themselves as having a disability. The college environment is generally far more accepting of differences than are most settings in the "real world." It is also generally more accessible than other environments. But despite federal and state legislation requiring that colleges and universities become accessible to the growing numbers of disabled students enrolling at mainstream schools, resources vary widely from school to school. Accommodations for students with disabilities range from accessible housing, to alternative testing conditions, to special visual aids, to cutting-edge computer technology that can help you write your papers or do your research. However, what is defined as "reasonable accommodations" can be murky—colleges are not required to provide accommodations that pose an "undue burden" to the institution—so it's important to find out what is likely to be offered to you at your particular school. If you have a disability, especially one that affects your mobility, you'll need to become familiar with how accessible your school is; if you can, visit the campus before you matriculate in order to get a clear sense of what sort of accommodations you'll require.

Whatever your particular disability is, check out your school's office of disabled student services; nearly every campus has one. In addition to coordinating the provision of reasonable accommodations and support services to students with disabilities, it also may provide personal, vocational, and peer counseling, as well as specialized tutoring and skill development for students with learning disabilities. Even if your school doesn't maintain an entire office, you should be able to locate counselors who can help you avoid unnecessary hassles and frustrations. And you should never hesitate to discuss a problem, particularly an accessibility problem, with your R.A., freshman counselor, or college dean.

If you have a disability that affects your mobility, consider disclosing that information to your college as soon as you accept their admissions offer. This will allow your school's housing gods to save you a place in an accessible building and assign you to an accessible dorm room. If you think that you'll need assistive technology, find out ahead of time, by talking to college administrators or other disabled students, whether the technology you need is available.

College is a uniquely rewarding time for all students, but if you're a student with a disability, college can represent a particular type of liberation: liberation from the notion that you are bound by the limitations of a disablity, and liberation from society's preconceived notions of what the lives of people with disabilities are like. Although you'll face challenges that students without disabilities won't share, for students with disabilities, college can be a crucial step towards independence and self-advocacy.

Conclusion

As second-semester seniors, my friends and I have started to wax nostalgic about our time at college. The consensus: We wish we had another four years, a chance to try new things, take a different path, or just do it all over again. It really does go by before you know it, just like everybody says.

So while you have the chance, take advantage of the unique social freedom of college life. Seize every academic opportunity that comes your way. Revel in your small victories and in your humiliating mistakes.

And above all, milk your college time for all the generally safe and mostly legal fun you can.

I hope you've gotten as much out of reading this book as I have out of writing it.

May the force be with you.

**For bulk sales to schools, colleges, and universities,
please contact:**

Renee Nemire
Simon & Schuster Special Markets
1633 Broadway, 8th Floor
New York, NY 10019.

come to us for the best prep

about KAPLAN

EDUCATIONAL CENTERS

"How can you help me?"

From childhood to adulthood, there are points in life when you need to reach an important goal. Whether you want an academic edge, a high score on a critical test, admission to a competitive college, funding for school, or career success, Kaplan is the best source to help get you there. One of the nation's premier educational companies, Kaplan has already helped millions of students get ahead through our legendary courses and expanding catalog of products and services.

"I have to ace this test!"

The world leader in test preparation, Kaplan will help you get a higher score on standardized tests such as the SSAT and ISEE for secondary school, PSAT, SAT, and ACT for college, the LSAT, MCAT, GMAT, and GRE for graduate school, professional licensing exams for medicine, nursing, dentistry, and accounting, and specialized exams for international students and professionals.

Kaplan's courses are recognized worldwide for their high-quality instruction, state-of-the-art study tools and up-to-date, comprehensive information. Kaplan enrolls more than 150,000 students annually in its live courses at 1,200 locations worldwide.

"How can I pay my way?"

As the price of higher education continues to skyrocket, it's vital to get your share of financial aid and figure out how you're going to pay for school. Kaplan's financial aid resources simplify the often bewildering application process and show you how you can afford to attend the college or graduate school of your choice.

KapLoan, The Kaplan Student Loan Information Program,° helps students get key information and advice about educational loans for college and graduate school. Through an affiliation with one of the nation's largest student loan providers, you can access valuable information and guidance on federally insured parent and student loans. Kaplan directs you to the financing you need to reach your educational goals.

"Can you help me find a good school?"

Through its admissions consulting program, Kaplan offers expert advice on selecting a college, graduate school, or professional school. We can also show you how to maximize your chances of acceptance at the school of your choice.

"But then I have to get a great job!"

Whether you're a student or a grad, we can help you find a job that matches your interests. Kaplan can assist you by providing helpful assessment tests, job and employment data, recruiting services, and expert advice on how to land the right job. Crimson & Brown Associates, a division of Kaplan, is the leading collegiate diversity recruiting firm helping top-tier companies attract hard-to-find candidates.

Kaplan has the tools!

For students of every age, Kaplan offers the best-written, easiest-to-use books. Our growing library of titles includes guides for academic enrichment, test preparation, school selection, admissions, financial aid, and career and life skills.

Kaplan sets the standard for educational software with award-winning, innovative products for building study skills, preparing for entrance exams, choosing and paying for a school, pursuing a career, and more.

Helpful videos demystify college admissions and the SAT by leading the viewer on entertaining and irreverent "road trips" across America. Hitch a ride with Kaplan's Secrets to College Admission and Secrets to SAT Success.

Kaplan offers a variety of services online through sites on the Internet and America Online. Students can access information on achieving academic goals; testing, admissions, and financial aid; careers; fun contests and special promotions; live events; bulletin boards; links to helpful sites; and plenty of downloadable files, games, and software. Kaplan Online is the ultimate student resource.

KAPLAN

Want more information about our services, products, or the nearest Kaplan educational center?

---- **HERE** ----

Call our nationwide toll-free numbers:

1–800–KAP–TEST
(for information on our live courses, private tutoring and admissions consulting)

1–800–KAP–ITEM
(for information on our products)

1–888–KAP–LOAN*
(for information on student loans)

Connect with us in cyberspace:

On **AOL**, keyword **"Kaplan"**

On the Internet's World Wide Web, open **"http://www.kaplan.com"**

Via E-mail, **"info@kaplan.com"**

Write to:
Kaplan Educational Centers
888 Seventh Avenue
New York, NY 10106